T0151018

the BOLD MANEUVER

the BOLD
MANEUVER

The Ambitious Woman's Playbook
for Achieving Greater Success

CALLIE CUMMINGS

NEW YORK

LONDON • NASHVILLE • MELBOURNE • VANCOUVER

the BOLD MANEUVER
The Ambitious Woman's Playbook for Achieving Greater Success

Published in New York, New York, by Morgan James Publishing in partnership with Difference Press. Morgan James is a trademark of Morgan James, LLC. www.MorganJamesPublishing.com

The Morgan James Speakers Group can bring authors to your live event. For more information or to book an event visit The Morgan James Speakers Group at www.TheMorganJamesSpeakersGroup.com.

ISBN 978-1-64279-136-5 paperback
ISBN 978-1-64279-137-2 eBook
Library of Congress Control Number: 2018948013

Cover Design by:
Rachel Lopez
www.r2cdesign.com

Interior Design by:
Bonnie Bushman
The Whole Caboodle Graphic Design

In an effort to support local communities, raise awareness and funds, Morgan James Publishing donates a percentage of all book sales for the life of each book to Habitat for Humanity Peninsula and Greater Williamsburg.

Get involved today! Visit
www.MorganJamesBuilds.com

To mother for making me the woman I am.

To my husband for being my rock and teammate
in this crazy ride, you are my everything.

TABLE OF CONTENTS

INTRODUCTION

Y ou've been working your buns off since the day you started your job. You searched for the right company, waited patiently for the right position to come open, jumped through all of the hiring hoops to finally land your dream job of the moment. It was the right fit at this point in your career. You took it knowing it would lead you to better opportunities of better pay and better positions down the road. Everything seemed to line up just the way you hoped it would. But now, you're a few years into the position and you're realizing the dream job is a B-I-G disappointment. You're not making the impact you think you should be making, and want to make. Your work is being undermined, someone else is taking credit for your ideas, you're pulling crazy hours unlike your teammates, and your promised time off and bonuses have been put on hold because there are other, more pressing, matters.

The real struggle though is feeling like you have to be someone other than yourself to get things done. Why is it that as a woman in the workforce if you're direct and assertive you're considered a bossy, but if you're easygoing and nice you get walked all over? You've tried both angles and both have failed miserably. And on top of that, neither one felt like you!

Then you have the good ol' boys club, which is very much a thing of the present, not the past... and the women around you rarely cheer each other on, instead cutting each other down. There seems to be no winning. University business classes somehow skipped over the whole office politics reality that somehow has the ability to make or break you. You're starting to realize why sitcoms like *The Office* are so popular. In fact, after your friend laughed at your last work story they suggested you watch a specific episode that depicted your exact situation. You were always good at building relationships, but somehow things just aren't clicking with your co-workers and you've realized you're in a constant state of self-doubt about how you interact at work.

The same comments run through your head every day,

"What am I doing wrong?"

"How could they promote him/her?"

"Maybe I should just quit."

This work scenario and feeling is way more common than you think. It isn't you, and you're definitely not alone in feeling this way. In fact, in a study done by Hunter College professor Pamela Stone, of 54 high-achieving women, 90% left their careers due to workplace problems. Crazy! Here you are feeling alone, and guilty for feeling the way you do, when in fact the majority of successful women feel the same way. You're either too bossy, too nice, too emotional, too this or too that. There seems to be no sweet spot for winning, for success.

It seems that women everywhere are missing a very important piece of knowledge. A piece so important that it's not only hindering their success, it's making them give up on their dreams.

What if I told you that this dilemma of workplace personality, balance of too nice and too bossy, is solvable? I mean there are thousands of examples of successful women making huge impacts across disciplines. They've uncovered the answer, but what is it and why is it not more widely known?

The truth is, there is no one solution that is a one-size-fits-all solution. People are complex, making the world we live in complex, and creating complex problems such as this. Women who have successfully found the solution to this problem have one thing in common whether they know it or not: they are strategists. They play a bigger-than-life chess game, they see systems everywhere they turn and identify opportunities and challenges, and make decisions from a strategic point of view. They have "rules" and/or "plays" that facilitate their movement through life.

Some people are inherently more strategic, and thus have an advantage to the complexity that we live in. In this book, I'm going to teach you how to become strategic in how you communicate and take action at the office. If you're scared by the word "strategy" or see it as a dirty word, the good news is that I am bringing it to you in a way that is digestible and exciting, and not only that, but strategy can be learned. This book is a playbook for very good reason. I want you to look at your work environment and problems as a game you're trying to win. If you're like me and you take life a little too seriously sometimes, a little game theory can lighten the load and help you conquer the ups and downs that come with real life and work.

I had always been one of those people who said, "I hate playing games." Life is not a game. I saw playing games as a negative and destructive means for bad people to run over good people. It took several years and a few wrong turns to realize that I had it all wrong. To make a difference, make an impact, create positive change and get ahead, you have to understand that they're playing a game with or without you, and they're playing to *win*. Winning could mean getting the next promotion, or being able to create a new team or new division, but you have to know that most people are playing the game of self-preservation.

We are all playing the game, you may not recognize it or don't want to admit to it, but I guarantee that you have multiple people currently playing the game against you, without you. If you're thinking to yourself that you're not competitive, or strategy seems a bit farfetched for you, I encourage you to remember why you picked up this book. You want to have success in your career and enjoy the journey, and what you've been doing hasn't been giving you the result you desire. If you want to achieve your goals, make a difference, and have success on your terms, then it's time to start making the necessary plays to get there, and this is exactly what this book is set up to do.

To achieve greatness in work and life we have to make bold maneuvers. To initiate change, we have to learn and execute the right plays. *The Bold Maneuver* is the strategy to push you through your career roadblocks through active initiative, and help you attain the success in your career that you've been striving for. It is named the Bold Maneuver because it takes courage, discipline, and boldness to shift how you perceive and react to the world around you. In the following chapters, you will uncover the six plays necessary to initiate and achieve the Bold Maneuver at work. **The One-on-One** will teach you why building relationships on an individual level with your co-workers is the key to deciphering personalities at work. **The Oprah** will provide strategies to create buy-in and influence from your peers and bosses that will make you more respected. **The Smarter, Not Harder** will reframe your perception of hard work to help you climb your corporate ladder. **The Alter Ego** will provide you a differing perspective and help you build your authentic work persona. **The Katniss** will help you increase your overall confidence or appearance of confidence to get things done. And **the Ice Princess** will help you understand how you're self-sabotaging your own success and how to overcome the mental blocks to change your habits.

Women have the ability to create change, and to make a better future for themselves and society; yet in so many cases women leave the corporate, non-profit, and government sectors before they make the difference they started out to make. The frustration and office politics often leave them feeling like they're on a mission impossible. This playbook is designed to help you stay on your path through all of the ups and downs so you can achieve the leadership positions and create the change you started out to make. The Bold Maneuver requires you to be bolder than you think you are, and more importantly, bolder than everyone else thinks you are.

The Story of Ice Princess

I always imagined myself one day being in a powerful position within the government or a large corporation. As a little girl I would see women in business suits with pin stripes and shoulder pads and be in awe of the power I thought they (must have) held. This may seem odd to some, most children have dreams of a specific job that they grow in and out of as they mature: a gymnast, a police officer, a marine biologist.... I, however, always knew I wanted to lead. Now, I obviously didn't know the full extent of what a leader was when I was younger, I just knew I wanted to be one. In this third-grade photo of me you can see how I fashioned myself after these women.

My mother still laughs at the fact that I would not budge when it came to this outfit choice. Look at those pink pin stripes and that bow tie broach! I just had to wear this for picture day! My entire life I have made decisions, sacrificed, and worked hard toward my desire to be a leader. I started working in business at the age of 14 hoping to get a head start in experience. I diversified my experience when I was young, from working in pharmaceutical inventory to grocery store customer service, from a government-run senior program to a large law firm, all before the age of 20. All in an attempt to gain experience from a young age to build me into my dream of being that "leader."

Coming out of university, I knew that I needed to go directly into grad school and continue my education to be eligible for future leadership opportunities. I had been working two to three jobs since I was 18, so I thought my work experience was good, but it would be helpful to have the higher education to go with it. It was fairly early in my master's when I realized there was a huge discrepancy between what we were learning about leadership (theory) and how it is actually applied (practice). In theory, leaders showed great idealism, positivity, kindness, and directness. In practice, leadership is much more muddled. A tactic that works on one person to push them to the next level, rarely works on another. So much of what is taught in theory is statistics and averages, but in leadership practice so much of success is based on your ability to lead personalities. No matter your gender, being a manager and/or leader is tricky business. The gap between leadership theory and practice is wide because in universities we are taught to be idealists, and then we graduate and move into our first job and realize the realists rule the day.

Whether you're in a worker bee position or a management position, at the end of the day your goal is what mine was, you want to be a leader. Leaders create change, and you want to be that change agent to make a positive difference. Understanding the gap between leadership theory and leadership practice is the first step to getting in the game.

In all of my work experience up to graduating with a master's, I had never really had any issues at work. I was a worker bee, I knew what I was, I was told what to do and did it. It wasn't until I started looking for growth opportunities as I started my career that I felt like something was off; something was different. My second job out of grad school was a United States Army officer. I learned very quickly in this male-dominant profession that "being me" wasn't going to make me successful. Anything feminine about me, personality or demeanor, was going to work against me and not for me.

There is a story that sticks out in my mind when I decided to join the army. It was with a friend who had been a marine while I was at university. He was talking me through my officer application and said, "Women are looked at as two things in the Marines, probably the same for the army. You're either a b**** or a whore. You can wait and have someone label you as one, or you can decide which one you want to be. Perception is reality, and if they perceive you as being a whore, you might as well forget even going in."

That conversation made a huge imprint on my years in the army. To my surprise for the four years of my military service there was an underlying struggle between the perception of b**** or whore. My colleague could be the biggest prick you've ever encountered and everyone thought he was the greatest for it, he was a true leader. If I was direct and passionate, I was considered a stuck-up princess.

In my first year in the army, I had to attend an engineering school for my job. I was placed in a leadership position toward the end of school, and during this period I was nicknamed "Ice Princess" by a peer for being cold-hearted and ruthless. I had simply done the same thing everyone else had done, but it was "different" with me. Had I not been no-nonsense and direct, I would have been walked all over and seen as weak.

It was at this point, early in my military career, that I started thinking, "How much of a jerk do I have to be to be successful?" If I could figure this out, I could make my mark, I could be that big corporate executive or politician I had always wanted to be. I made this question my personal mission. No matter what situation I was in, what organization I was with, or where I was, I made decisions and moves to solve this question. The answer wasn't what I thought it would be, and after many years of struggling, fighting the fight, and self-doubt, I realized I wasn't the problem, my outlook on the problem was my problem.

Let The Chips Fall

The Ice Princess story from above is only the beginning to that story. My first realization about my outlook came several years after when I realized I had a chip on my shoulder. That conversation with my friend telling me I could choose "b***" or whore" made me view almost every situation as me vs. them, men vs. women, and it was self-sabotaging. I felt like every day was a fight. A fight over ego, a fight over fairness, a fight over perception. Every day felt like I was fighting my way through. And what I couldn't understand, was that I was living in the twenty-first century, shouldn't the fight be over? At least that's what I thought when I entered the professional world. The issue was that subconsciously I was seeing every situation as a me-versus-them scenario. And while some situations were very much a gender issue, most of them were not. Most of the situations were personality differences, cultural differences, but with that chip on my shoulder, I limited my ability to see the real causes and symptoms.

When assessing situations, I thought I was being strategic, but my subconscious chip was limiting my depth of understanding. I felt like I was in middle school all over again with the office politics. I felt like I was set up for failure thinking the fight for fairness was over and done, and all I had to do was show up and work hard. You, like me, were likely told that if you work hard and do the right thing, you'll be successful and have everything you want in life. You've likely already come to terms with that wonderful notion not being reality. Whether you have a similar chip on your shoulder, or a different one, no matter what the reason, it is important to identify it and let it roll off. It will sabotage your ability to grow in your career because you're unable to solve problems at their roots.

The Plan vs. Reality

Remember how I said life is complex and your problem is more common than you think? Well, I am no exception to either of these things. My life has been a rollercoaster of sorts, one that has put me through the ringer of ups and down, joy and sadness. You've likely seen this picture below. The depiction of how you imagine things to go, and how they actually go, well... this has been my path through life.

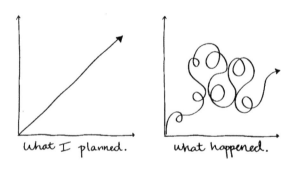

what I planned.   what happened.

This is one of my favorite illustrations of life. So simple, yet so true. It is a picture that some may loath or cringe at when recognizing its truth, but I get a little giggle every time I see it. I am reminded of how my experiences, both planned and unexpected, have shaped me. I've always known what I wanted to be, but the path to get there was much different than I could have ever imagined.

No matter what you do or how much you try, some things will simply be out of your control. Your path will be much different than you planned, or even imagined, but the more prepared you are for the out-of-control, the more adept you'll be at outmaneuvering the crazy unexpected twists and turns.

There are three rules that I live by:

- S*** Happens
- Life's Not Fair
- No One Owes You Anything

You may be thinking, wow, that is a negative outlook on life! But is it? Have you ever said, "stuff happens!"? What about, "this isn't fair!"? Or, have you expected someone to pull through, and they fall short? If you think about it, when stuff happens, life's not fair, and no one is there to help, are you going to be ready to put one foot in front of the other, and go? These rules are a perfect place to start in shifting your outlook. There is something refreshing about accepting these three rules. If you can internalize these three rules, and make them your go-to mantra when stuff happens and life's not fair, your entire perception on whatever struggles you're having will shift. You will begin to laugh off those things that tore at you for years. What this is doing is mentally conditioning you for when things are out of your control. Coming back to these rules will help you continue to move forward without getting too far off track before you're too far gone.

I must warn you, there are hundreds of personal growth and performance books on the market today that provide a comforting tone of warm and fuzzy motivation; as you've likely discerned already, this is not one of those books. We've gradually moved into a society that quotes, posts, and talks in landscape images with cursive writing and motivational words, none of which will actually change your life. No service is done by creating an alternative reality; that has been done enough from our childhoods of just work hard and do the right thing. I will provide you the real, raw, complex reality, with full transparency so you are able to make the impact you were meant to make.

The Bold Maneuver

Everyone starts out their career with an end state in mind. Mine was to be a leader, a leader that helped people. Think about what yours was when you started college. It may have shifted over the years as you've grown and matured, but what is your goal for your career? I want you to make a note of this to reference while you're reading this book.

Your end state may be personal, maybe it's for your community, or society as a whole. It may be for monetary gains, or societal gains. No matter what it is,

I bet your end state has something to do with making a positive impact.

The first lesson in the Bold Maneuver is to understand you've got to play the game. You cannot make that positive difference, impact, change, and get ahead, if people around you are playing without you. They're playing a game with or without you and they're playing to *win*.

The second lesson in the Bold Maneuver is to find love in the game. If you're reading this, it is because you want to go further and higher than your current status. You may be frustrated, struggling, or maybe even ready to walk away. The good news is, all of these negative feelings can be shifted just a bit and help you enjoy the journey ahead no matter what twists and turns may come.

I grew up playing a multitude of sports, from basketball, volleyball, ice skating, tai kwon do, to even being a pole vaulter. What I liked most about sports wasn't the competition or the physicality. I preferred to play for the fun and friendship, than for the win. For me, it was always the strategy that intrigued me. How an underdog in athleticism could win if they were a better strategist than a physically dominant specimen of a human that didn't mentally play the game. I had to make up for my lacking in a few areas with strengths in another. Have you ever thought about how much sport teams and universities pay for their coaching staff? They spend so much effort and money on coaching staff to ensure they have the best strategists available. Each year a team has different players, some come on and others leave. This means that a team never really knows what the dynamics of their team is going to be as far as players go; therefore, if the team lacks the physical or mental capacity against the competition, a good coach can devise a strategy that plays to their strengths for the win.

The Center for American Progress reported in 2017 that in the S&P 500 Labor Force women make up just 36 percent of first- or mid-level officials and managers, 25 percent of executive- and senior-level officials and managers, 20 percent of board seats, and 6 percent of CEOs. Proof that we are still living and working in a man's world. This is something that you may not want to hear, but the statistics say it all. And if we are working in a man's world, to *win* at their game, we must play it better than them. They have a competitive drive that puts Darwin's Theory of "survival of the fittest" into play. In this point of view, they don't admit or recognize they're even playing a game. When you come to realize that you're playing against Darwin's Theory, it will be so relieving. It isn't us vs. them, it's just nature. All this time you thought the issue was you. You thought the problem at work was your fault. The truth is, you are not making the difference you want, achieving the success you hoped for, and enjoying the journey because you're fighting against nature.

I want to help you learn to love the game, love the challenge. In this way we have to change how you perceive and move through the game of life. Being bold does not mean having to be a jerk or power-hungry. The definition of bold is being courageous or daring, not hesitating to move forward. Being bold is moving beyond conventional action. The Bold Maneuver is you taking action in a new way to achieve new and improved results. No matter the situation, only you can take action to make you successful.

In the book you will hear me talk about end states. I am not just talking about a promotion. End states can be getting someone to be more participatory. Having someone successfully execute a task. Improving motivation within a team or department, or completing a large project. End states do not specifically benefit you, they benefit the organization. It is important to recognize this difference. The goal is to move up the corporate ladder successfully, but this is done through the successful accomplishment of everyday tasks, and being part of a cohesive team helps you to accomplish that without doing it all on your own.

I have named each play in the playbook to represent a specific attitude and/or behavior. You will see opportunities all around you to play the game now that you realize there is a game to be played. Instead of trying to recall an entire play at every opportunity, I have purposefully used trigger words to subconsciously cue you as to which play to play.

You will likely use the first play in the Bold Maneuver, **the One-on-One,** the most. This play can be equated to playing one-on-one in a basketball game. You have to guard your opponent from scoring, and to do so you must learn how they move, which hand is their dominant, what their go-to moves are. It is important to recognize that people view themselves as an individual, not a generalization or stereotype. We live and do things based on our personal experiences, and getting to know the psychology of people helps you learn how to leverage their positive and negative qualities to better position yourself. You'll use this play about half the time both at work and in regular life situations that deal with people. No one ever told me how important relationships were to my success, it is a lesson I wished I had learned earlier. If you listen to the top business people around the world, you will hear that they had the dream and the drive but they didn't do it alone. If you are thinking, I was taught to be independent, you are just like me. I can't wait to help you uncover the power behind the One-on-One.

The second play, **the Oprah**. Named for the one and only Oprah Winfrey, who can be best characterized as one of the greatest influencers of our time. It takes the One-on-One and leverages the relationship you built to create influence within your organization. Influence is one of the more difficult plays to master. You know the saying, "it takes two to tango." Creating influence is a two-sided relationship; it will take time to build it out. You are looking for champions within and outside your organization that will advocate for your elevation. It takes consistency and dedication to prove to them that you are worth their reputation of championing you.

The Smarter, Not Harder is one of the more fun and interesting plays in the Bold Maneuver. You were likely told the majority of your life that working hard was enough. Unfortunately, that is a fable in the real world. The Smarter Not Harder is about finding and leveraging efficiency, learning to be adaptable in any situation, and learning to think about the world around you systemically. When you're able to think in systems, conveniently called systems thinking, you will begin to see the multitude of systems around you running congruently, exposing leverage points to create efficient and effective outcomes. No matter what, all business leaders are looking for results. If you are able to deliver these in a more efficient and effective manner than anyone else, you will prove your invaluableness in a way that you've never experienced.

In the fourth play, **the Alter Ego**, you will begin to uncover that answer to "how much of a jerk do I have to be to be successful." Unfortunately, one of the other lies we've been told about success is that we must present our authentic self all the time to bring internal happiness and outward success. What this "authentic self" narrative gets wrong is that we have multiple authentic selves. You will learn how to leverage your work persona and balance the hard and soft sides of your personality to achieve success.

The Katniss play is one that most people, including my past self, make their primary play. The Katniss is about embracing your inner confidence like never before. The reason most women fail at this play is because they focus on trying to answer, "how much of a jerk do I have to be to be successful." They focus so much of their time on being fierce and trying to one up everyone else, they miss the point that the Katniss isn't about anyone else, it's about you. This play will help you learn to internalize your inner power and leverage that confidence toward your other plays.

The hardest play in the playbook is **the Ice Princess**. In the time of social media, where we are in an intense state of judging and judgment, the days of the middle school tragedy can become a constant state. That judgment state of mind easily spills over into every other aspect of life, including work. In the Ice Princess you will learn to turn off your judgment state of mind to enable an empathetic state of mind, and turn off the fear of being judged. So much of why you're not finding the success you want is because you're afraid of what others will think if you do this or that. You are in a cyclical state of analysis paralysis over someone else's judgment. I refer to Eleanor Roosevelt's quote for this play, "Do what you feel in your heart to be right - for you'll be criticized anyway. You'll be damned if you do, and damned if you don't." It's time to turn that wasted energy over to the other plays.

To find success with the Bold Maneuver plays, there is one more aspect we have to address, and that is Functional Fitness. It isn't enough just to be good at the plays, you'll need to have strengths behind the play, this is what keeps you bold when you're feeling like going back to your regular habits. In this chapter I will cover how mental, emotional, and physical fitness play into the Bold Maneuver and your overall career success. Functional Fitness elements provide the foundation to play the plays.

In learning to love the game, we have to learn to turn your opponent into an ally. This may sound like an odd concept considering most of our lives we've been taught that our opponent is the enemy; however, this is the essential element that will be the difference to your success or continued struggle. Most of us look at the opponent in this situation as the jerk boss, or the egotistical co-worker, but the real opponent is the real world. We like to live in a reality of peace and security, but the real world doesn't function in that reality. You will learn to understand how living in a sheltered mentality is hindering your success, and how to make the real world your ally instead of your foe.

THE ONE-ON-ONE

How well do you know the people around you? Your spouse, your significant other, your co-workers, your friends? Do you know why they think, react, and do the things they do? Personality psychology is understanding the core of why people think, feel, and act, and it is the premise of the One-on-One. The reason we want to learn about how and why someone thinks the way they do is because it helps us determine how to react to them and position our communication in a way that achieves the best result. Remember, being bold is taking unconventional action; if you are trying to achieve exceptional results within a team for a promotion, or be seen as a leader beyond your current scope, effective communication is a crucial element.

Most leadership and management books taught in universities, and leadership articles written for business professionals, don't touch enough on personality types. We are all asked at some point or another to take the Meyers-Briggs personality assessment to help us become more self-aware of who we are and why we think the way we do. In some cases you may learn the difference between the different personality types of the assessment. But what is missing is why it is important. Leadership and management books teach us to focus on the economics of people, the median, the average, in other words the stereotype when we're making decisions. In theory, looking at the average of our environment makes sense because that means we are able to hit the majority of people we connect with. In practice, going for the median can be a huge detriment to your relationships with people and further to your success. People don't look at themselves as the average person, we all think of ourselves as individuals, a unique individual. We all come from different pasts, different experiences, different backgrounds, all of which make us who we are.

Personality tests are a great surface level tool to help with self-awareness and understanding different ways in which people think, but what it can't do and we must is go deeper into what experiences created the personality we're dealing with. Knowing that experiences created the personalities we're dealing with makes it easier to pinpoint where you can best influence them. If you feel your co-worker is not stepping up to their role, understanding their perspective, their past work experience, their relationship with other team members, will help you understand where you can most effect and influence their behavior. If you took the Meyers-Briggs personality assessment in high school, it is likely that your results were much different then than they are today. In a peer reviewed scientific study of genetics, twins were studied to determine how much of their personality was the result of heredity and environment. Results showed that anywhere between 61-82% of an individual's personality traits come from the environment, circumstances, and personal experiences.

Whether you're a worker bee or in a leadership position, becoming proficient in personality psychology will prove to be paramount in your ability to gain respect, trust, and influence. My husband laughs every time I meet someone new because more often than not, I learn their very personal life stories within our first encounter. Okay, maybe not their entire life story, but a good piece of it. He's mesmerized by what people will tell me without really knowing me, both men and women. The play is the One-on-One. I have learned to listen to people at their level and am open to understanding where they come from. This can be related to the active listener or the empathetic listener skills.

The One-on-One play in the workplace can mean the difference between being average and being high-caliber. You've likely picked up this book because you're struggling with a relationship(s) in the office. You've attempted several things to make it better: being nicer, being more helpful, giving them praise, being less vocal, creating small talk... All of these are Band-Aid methods.

One-on-one is the symptom method. With knowledge of personal psychology, active listening, and empathetic listening you will be able to play the One-on-One effectively. Depending on the person you're trying to get to know, it can take a few hours or even a few months. It can only be done through authentic and genuine conversation. But in your first few real conversations with them you will be able to piece together small nuggets of how and why they think and do what they do. You are not trying to make everyone your best friends. Building a personal and genuine rapport with someone will help you leverage what you know about them to better communicate with them so you can achieve the end state you're working toward.

When I left the army and went back into the corporate sector, I got what seemed like a dream job in a dream company. Within the first few weeks of my employment, a co-worker asked me if I noticed how my boss talked to me. She was several years older than me and started several weeks after I did, but how our direct supervisor talked to me was much different than how he talked to everyone else, and we both noticed! For the next year I dealt with a condescending tone and jokes about me reminding him of his fourteen-year-old daughter. Mind you, this was with a master's degree, four years of leadership in the United States Army, and being one of the first in a group of women to lead an all-male combat force during a time of war. Had his fourteen-year-old daughter done any of these things? Didn't my experience and my everyday work prove I was not equitable to a teenager? I had approached him several times about the relation to his daughter feeling like an insult, yet the comments continued. This was literally a dream job for me, and I let someone push me out after 16 months because I didn't know how to deal with the condescension and insults. I let someone determine my path for me. I didn't understand until my outgoing interview and conversations with my co-workers that he was upset I was leaving and was remorseful for making me feel like I had no option but to leave. I took his comments and tone toward me as insults, where he thought he was being endearing. This entire time we were miscommunicating, and I was assuming his intention. Similar to this experience, in other situations, I felt like I was fighting my way to the top and was miserable. I wanted to learn how to be in situations that were uncomfortable or irritable, yet come away every day from work and feel good. This experience showed me I was in some cases getting in my own way. I let my ego and emotions drive my reactions. There was nothing that boss did that set my career back, in fact he was very positive in wanting me to succeed. Instead of learning where his comments and behavior were coming from, I removed myself from the game due to irritation. Had I played the One-on-One I would have discovered that we simply had different communication styles and it was possible to adjust how we communicated, and build a closer and better relationship; but instead I left that position and a dream job.

Office Personalities

When you start to understand how and why people work, you will find that there are some circumstances that you can and cannot juggle. Co-workers with personality disorders can create a draining and toxic work environment. This can impede your own productivity at the office or even permeate into your home life. They can stall entire teams as everyone tries to contain the chaos. As I mentioned in the beginning of the chapter, understanding personalities and personality traits will be a game changer. It is the difference in knowing whether to keep moving forward or move away.

We all have them, they're in every office in America. They may be your co-worker, your subordinate, or your leadership, but they are everywhere. The few that I will mention are the egomaniac, the drama queen, the lazy individual, and the sociopath. We'll go through each one and work through how to outmaneuver them with the One-on-One.

The Egomaniac

Almost everyone has self-interest or self-seeking purposes in what they're doing. Everyone wants better hours, better pay, or better relationships with the boss; this is normal. Excessive self-interest and ego is where the majority of your problems lie. In this book you are learning how to leverage relationships for your benefit; this is self-interest. What I am not teaching you is how to run over people and negate morality or ethics in your end state of success. The latter is the excess. I didn't understand this difference in my twenties, and had I, my life may have had a very different path.

A lot of people are taught that ego is a bad thing and it is not justified. Whether that is your religious, spiritual, or ethical teachings, most of us have a negative connotation of ego. If we look at personal goals however, most can be traced back to our egos. Having an ego is not bad, being egotistical to the detriment of others is. Most people are the former and not the latter, but there will be about a quarter of people in your organization who are the latter. When dealing with these people, the personality psychology comes in handy. To outmaneuver someone's ego you must understand its purpose. Again, we are trying to leverage their ego, to help us accomplish a goal. Your goal can be as simple as ensuring they do their job so you're not having to, or as complex as preventing them from walking all over other teammates or yourself. Sometimes this will result in praise or flattery, other times it will result in directness and firmness. We must learn how to be effective communicators, especially to the egotistical personalities, to better position ourselves to achieve an end state. In fact, in my story about my condescending boss, it was my own ego that got in my way. I let my ego of my experiences and education get in the way of understanding where he was coming from, and I took his comments personally and reacted through assumption.

The Drama Queen

Then there are people who thrive on drama. This can be detrimental to you and your team's productivity. People who thrive on drama can fall into the Histrionic Personality Disorder. They affect 2-3% of the population and can be just as difficult to outmaneuver due to their unstable emotional state. In some cases, those who seek drama don't intend to be malicious they're just dramatic. In these cases, simply excusing yourself or reacting with lack of emotion can easily blow out a spark. Have you ever had someone come at you very upset and you simply pretended like they're not upset and continued on? It stops them in their tracks, they do not know how to respond, because they're used to drama in return.

Lazy

If you're finding yourself at the office, by yourself, for the third time this week, it's likely due to you having a lazy person on your team. This person can also be described as someone not pulling their weight. Sometimes it is simply a different work ethic to yours, and they refuse to pull after hours as it's against everything they believe in. And sometimes people work harder finding ways not to do their job than actually doing their job.

The lazy person may not be a toxic personality or be a disruption within the team or department, but they can make your life much more difficult. In some instances their laziness may be true laziness or it may be a side effect of something else. It could be that they are truly poor at time management, or prioritization, and it is a skill set issue. In this instance, you or your boss can easily suggest some tools. In other areas, they may only work on one level, and that pace is not in line with the project or the team. In this instance, it is just good to know ahead of time if they are less productive due to pace so you set your expectations of performance accordingly. Not everyone has the same capacity, and it may seem unfair that not everyone is at your level when you're hired for the same position and pay. Unfortunately, you will come across this a lot, and it is just easier to understand someone's capacity and intention. Then there are those people who seem to have the perfect scam going. They never seem to get their work done and it always falls on someone else, and it's not that they don't have the capacity or they're lacking in a skill, it's that they don't have the motivation to be there. With this personality the buy-in is oh so important. We will talk about influence and buy-in in the next chapter, and you will start to understand how each play supports the other, but with this person you have to understand how to motivate them and leverage that to create a fire under them to do their job at the level it needs to be done.

Sociopath

In *The Sociopath Next Door*, Dr. Martha Stout suggests that 1 in 25 people, 4 percent of the population, are sociopaths. In personality disorders such as the sociopath, you will not be able to outmaneuver this person because the definition of sociopath defines them as lacking a conscience. Their self-interest and self-preservation to get ahead will occur by any means necessary. If you're up against an office sociopath it is necessary to assess if leaving is the better option. It depends on what level you're at, versus the co-worker whom you're having issues with. Unfortunately, with sociopaths their lack of moral or ethical boundaries will always outplay you. Because they don't have a code of conduct, you will find it much harder to leverage them in a positive direction.

THE GOAL

As you start to learn more and more about someone it is important to not make large assumptions with a few pieces. This is where I've had clients veer off course into a dangerous area. The intent here is not to amateurishly diagnose people. The intent is to understand the intent of others. There is a difference in malicious intent and miscommunication. A lot of negative interactions with people are simple cases of miscommunication. This is why having a state of empathy, lack of instant judgment, less emotional reaction, and asking people what they mean are so important. We can end up creating a lot of unnecessary effort because we didn't know intent. In some cases there is malicious intent, and in these cases you will have to assess if the One-on-One or even the Bold Maneuver will be beneficial; sometimes walking away is your only option. I have had many clients say they have walked away thinking it was the only option, but if they had known then what they know now, and had used the One-on-One, they say they could have attained more success staying where they were and playing the game.

THE OPRAH

As Oprah Winfrey is one of the most influential women in the United States, it makes perfect sense that the chapter on creating influence would be named after her. Achieving great success is rarely a singular effort. Anyone who has an empire will be the first to tell you that they didn't create it on their own. They worked hard, harder than the average, but working hard wasn't enough. They had a team, they had mentors, and they had investors. And to get a team, mentors, and investors they had to learn to create influence and buy-in so people were willing to support them and their goals. When you think about how you're going to accomplish your goals, I want you to think of the Oprah play.

Oprah is the expert of influence because she's been creating it for most of her life. What most people don't know about her story is that she started addressing congregations and giving speeches at social gatherings from the age of 12. While in her teens, she took advantage of any opportunity she had to speak to people, participating in drama club, debate club, student council, speaking competitions, and local radio station newscasts. From there she went on to work as a news broadcaster, anchor, actress, production company CEO, and, well, you know the rest of the story.

I am not going to attempt to teach you everything Oprah knows about influence, because that is a lifetime of lessons that only she can teach. This chapter will cover three components of someone starting to look at influence as a foundation block to success.

It All Begins With Gratitude

Has anyone ever told you that what you really need to do is be grateful? All of the really famous life coaches preach gratitude like we're a bunch of unappreciative degenerates. If you're like me, when you hear "be grateful" you immediately brush it off... because you are grateful. Or so you think you are.

You were brought up with morals, and parents or grandparents who taught you to say thank you. You understand what it means to have more than others, and you give back in little ways hoping to show that you are thankful for all of the great things you have in life. But this isn't the gratitude people are talking about when they say, "be grateful."

It wasn't until I was 30 and in my second year in Afghanistan, which has one of the most impoverished populations in the world, that I had a light bulb moment about gratitude. There is a much deeper level of gratitude that these experts are speaking of, that goes beyond being thankful for the things we have. The best way for me to explain it is to use the word compromise. When most people think of gratitude at work they think of the good parts, the easy parts, being grateful to have a good team or a great boss. Gratitude on the new scale occurs when you can't see the good in something. At work, compromise can be one of the most dreaded words. We understand that working with others means that we are not the primary concern. Your ideas, your goals, and your feedback are amongst a group of ideas, goals, and feedback. We all tend to have a hidden ego that makes us want to get our way. You have formed habits over the last 20+ years, and you have specific ways of approaching a situation or solving a problem. When you become a member of a team, the consensus rules, or sometimes an authority rules. This means that the habits you've formed through your trials and tribulations, the life tested strategies and solutions can be overruled by what seems to be a less efficient and effective idea. Compromise can seem like the ugly part of work, but with gratitude we make it positive. In this example, true gratitude is being thankful for the opportunity to learn, the opportunity to choose between multiple ways. In the army there is a saying, "You learn just as much from a bad leader as you do from a good leader, because with a bad leader you learn what not to do." The end state of the compromise becomes less important, and the recognition of options becomes the gift. Compromise is no longer seen as antagonistic, but an advantage. Mastering gratitude, being grateful, is being able to see past ego and pride and into the condition.

The reason influence begins with gratitude is because you are essentially asking for more. You are asking others to invest their time, their thoughts, their money, their reputation in you. And for people to be willing to help you, whether it be for a project task or for $1 million, they need to feel that you are deserving. Being humble and grateful go hand in hand here. People want to help people they deem worthy.

The definition of influence is "the capacity or power to be a compelling force on or produce effects on the actions, behavior, and opinions of others." Creating influence is leveraging someone's emotion to benefit a specific outcome. In your situation you will need to create influence within your team so they are willing to become active participants. You will need to create influence with your higher-ups so they are willing to promote you. You will need to create influence across different departments so they are willing to combine efforts toward a larger purpose. The list can go on and on.

The ability to create influence will be the make it or break it fundamental. No one can do everything on their own, and you shouldn't want to. You are likely stressed out right now because you feel like you are doing it on your own. If you had the buy-in and influence from your co-workers they wouldn't push their work off on you. If you had the buy-in from your leadership, they would take your recommendations and run with them. For anyone to want to change their actions for you though, you need to make them feel like they want to help you. Showing humility, humbleness, and gratefulness will make people want to invest in you.

Vulnerability

If you remember back in the One-on-One I told you that people tend to share very deep and personal details about their lives with me; anyone who has mastered this skill will tell you that it comes out of vulnerability. Not only does this skill require genuine interest in others, but being able to be vulnerable with a complete stranger.

Vulnerability is a feeling you likely shy away from. It has become a word for weakness and failure in our society, and if you show vulnerability you will more than likely be labeled these things. This stigma could not be further from the truth. What people connect with is realness. Who doesn't feel uncomfortable and unsure, or hasn't failed at something or made mistakes? People can relate to you when you're normal. Our society has centered around perfectionism in the age of social media, but while perfection is great from a distance it is not something anyone can relate to because no one is perfect. Artificial perfection is fun to look at from a distance, but makes people feel like failures in real life and is a huge turn-off.

Do you remember watching Jennifer Lawrence fall up the stairs to get her Oscar? How vulnerable was that moment! The biggest moment in your life, something you never thought you'd achieve, then actually did, and the whole world watches you fall as you take the most defining steps in your career. I don't know about you but I didn't feel sorry for her. I didn't see her fall as embarrassing as much as I did relatable. I almost fell through the cathedral doors at my wedding when my foot got caught inside my hoop skirt. While she was a popular actress long before that moment, that moment of vulnerability made her a household name.

When striving to create influence with anyone, your boss, or your boss' boss, your co-workers, or executives, being genuine and real is an understated quality today. Leaders want to know that they have people who are going to be honest in hard situations, learn from their mistakes, and be a team player. Being vulnerable means that you allow people to see your failures, your struggles, and your flaws. What so many people do with this move, though, is go overboard with reality. You know that saying "No one wants to see how the sausage is made"? Well, that can be the same for realness. No one wants every intricate detail of your life, your missteps and your drama. In your profession, your team and your bosses want you to bring the best version of you to the team. Delivery is the key component to mastering vulnerability.

When you're working on being vulnerable with someone, just remember your photo filters. Photo filters aren't supposed to be photoshopped, the goal is not to take out or hide something in the picture. The goal is to make a shadow a little less harsh or light a little more vibrant. You're not trying to change the reality, just adjust the tones. The same rule goes for being vulnerable. You must be genuine without being fake. Filters are still real, just an adjusted delivery. Photoshop is fake, and not reality.

It Takes A Village

I'd be surprised if you didn't hear the saying "It takes a village to raise a child," when you were younger. Raising children who are kind, moral, and resilient has to be the toughest thing a person can undertake. It helps when you have grandparents close by who can babysit, after-school programs so parents can work full time, and extracurricular activities for further development, all of which is your extended community coming together to mentor your child in different environments and phases. "It takes a village." I remember hearing quite a lot, and it is unfortunately something we're now missing in a lot of our communities.

With young people moving across the state, across the country, or to other countries, we're not staying in the communities that we grew up in. I left Missouri when I was 18 to move to Hawai'i where I knew *no one*. Globalization has provided us an opportunity to spread our wings and explore the world, but there are downsides, and loss of long-term community ties is one of them. While you may have a good group of friends and acquaintances in your new hometown, you just don't have that rooted community connection. The reason this is so important is because your teachers, your parents' friends, your friends' parents have all become the senior community members, board members and business executives. These are the people who feel invested in your success because they were part of your development. As you start looking for new opportunities, these are the people who can help provide them or the connections to them. While you can certainly be successful without "the village" as an adult, the longer you do it alone, the more you'll realize how much connections are worth.

People invest in people/places/things they know intimately. They know that there is a return on investment in some manner. If you are like me and are without community ties as an adult, it is imperative to start making the effort to build them. I wish it hadn't taken me so long to figure this out. I was so independent, I never wanted to have to count on anyone, so I never fully became invested in the communities in which I lived. What I was really doing though was sabotaging future opportunities for people to invest in me, because they didn't know me.

Now if you know you are going to constantly move like me—12+ times in the decade following high school—the local community may not be the place where you need to invest. Associations and communities associated with your career may be a better opportunity. What has become really popular with social media is becoming involved in communities where the majority of the members are of similar age demographics, but when you're looking at influence, you need to become involved in the older demographics. You want people who are power players and established to be your mentors and champions. We like to think that older generations are less capable because they are less tech savvy, but their experiences, resources, and connections are something technology can't provide at the human level.

You must create your village as an adult to create influence. Building "tribes" has become a more recent concept with a similar outcome in mind. Whether it's a village or a tribe, having a community that feels invested in your success and is willing to support you in any way possible is paramount to your growth potential.

THE GOAL

There are many reasons for you to have influence and buy-in, but in your situation right now, the most likely reason is because your boss or your co-workers are working against you. When you have people who are standing in the way of your success because of their incompetence, their personal feelings, bias, or perception, it can feel like a no-win situation. Creating influence outside of your immediate team helps build your reputation. Creating influence requires you to be good at your job, be dedicated, and hard working, it doesn't come without the core foundations. Gratitude and vulnerability set the conditions for influence, it isn't created by itself. Your reputation right now may be based on someone else's influence, but the goal is to have your reputation based on your influence.

THE SMARTER, NOT HARDER

You've heard it before, Smarter, Not Harder, but what does it really mean? You're obviously a hard worker, otherwise you wouldn't have picked up this book, and you consider yourself to be smart, so how are you not already working smarter not harder? Working smarter, not harder in this chapter encompasses three key principles: hard work, efficiency, and adaptability. As these principles support the foundation of the Smarter, Not Harder, they are referred to here as pillars.

In this new era of ever-changing technology, where yesterday's breakthroughs are old news, working hard is simply not enough anymore. Technology has changed the way we work and play. As young adults, our parents and teachers taught us that working hard is the key component to success. While they had the best intentions, this notion is outdated in our current society. In order to create job security and increase your promotion timeline, you must prove yourself to be irreplaceable. Smarter, Not Harder is about outmaneuvering candidates for your current and future opportunities. If your goal is to keep moving up the ladder, reach higher salaries, attain management positions, and be a leader inside and outside your organization, you must show you have the capacity to not only work hard, but work smart.

Pillar 1: Hard Work

If you were thinking that if hard work isn't the be-all and end-all, and that I'm going to give you a shortcut, I'm sorry to let you down. Your work ethic is still going to be a pillar of what sets you apart, it doesn't fall off with smarter not harder. The goal is to not work harder than everyone else. In the One-on-One, I mentioned the lazy personality, the person who would rather work harder to find ways out of doing their job, than to actually do their job. These people look like they're hard workers because they're hard at work getting others to do their job and create their success. This is why hard work by itself is not enough, it does not set you apart. I have so many clients who when they first come to me believe they are productive and excellent time managers, yet they have so many frustrations about having to do several other people's work. This, my friend, is working harder. So many people find themselves in this situation. There are two reasons for this. One, they are afraid to say no for fear of not looking like a team player. Or two, they are genuinely nice people who want to help their colleague out. I am not saying that you should always say no when others ask for your help in regard to their work, this is team work. What I am saying is that more often than not, those few yeses turn into a second job. You find yourself not only doing your work but the majority of work for one or more people because they took that inch and ran a mile. Working smarter is being able to tell people no when they are trying to put their work on you. Working harder is why there is so much burnout. Initial acts of kindness turn into overwhelming workloads. Continue to have a great work ethic, and be a team player, but try to be conscious of how much you allow yourself to get involved in other people's work, for this will only mean you're working harder for someone else's gain.

Pillar 2: Efficiency

The definition of efficiency is improving performance to a desired result by avoiding waste. What will set you apart from everyone else is eliminating wasted time, efforts, energy, materials, and money from your work and your team's work. You probably think you're already efficient, and if that is the case you will have one less skill set to master. A test of this can be seen in how quickly you can perform a task compared to someone else of equal intelligence. Intelligence does not equal efficiency, intelligent people are not always efficient personalities. Have you ever had a co-worker who always had time during the day to slack off, because they completed all of their tasks for the day? These people likely set up a system for themselves to create efficiency within their work hours. Efficiency can be on a small or large scale. If you are looking to improve upon this skill set, I would first suggest starting with your personal daily productivity and start looking at ways to make it more efficient. In many cases people who try to create efficiency don't take the time to understand and analyze the symptoms of the problem they're trying to solve. In the army, these people are called good idea fairies. They come up with "great ideas," and get people excited, without understanding the full impact their suggested idea will have on the whole. In applying any skill, it is important to first crawl, then walk, then run. What most people want to do is solve the big problem for more attention and glory, and end up creating less efficiency because they never learned the basics of the skill.

Utilizing a thought process called systems thinking is the most practical tool in finding efficiency. Systems thinking is a way of taking the things around us, and turning them into parts that can be broken down, analyzed, and improved upon. The "improved upon" part is the efficiency, but that is the end state, not the starting point. When an improvement is applied without understanding the whole of a system, or the related systems that will be impacted, negative byproducts of an idea that started out to create "efficiency" begin to create different and/or larger problems. You can probably think of several examples of this occurring, someone on your team suggesting a great "fix" for an issue in your team meeting, and you're thinking they're crazy because they haven't accounted for some very clear pieces of the puzzle.

When I started working for Cisco, the high tech giant, they had a twelve-week in-processing program. I had never been responsible for my own in-processing before. Going into the army, it was very regimented. From the time I enlisted to making it to my first unit 18 months later, I had someone telling me where to be and what time to be there through any in-processing procedure. Feeling a bit out of my element, I decided to browse through each step of the process and make a to-do list of everything I needed to accomplish. I then made a list of every department and contact I was supposed to call, and scheduled meetings for every person over the next week. What I ended up doing was creating a process on top of their process that was more efficient for me to take action. Because I had scheduled all of the meetings in that first week, and didn't wait for those requirements to come up later in the process, I ended up completing the majority of the in-processing in three days, and completed all of the tasks within the first week. My boss and boss' boss had never seen someone do this before. The majority of the first six weeks of an employee was dedicated to in-processing. This meant that an employee wasn't really able to learn their job or help their team for the first month and a half of their employment. How annoying is that? The reason you hire someone is because you're in need of their skills and their work, but with their system they created a huge lag in the ability for someone to begin to learn. In my first week, I had set myself apart and made a positive impact on my new leadership. In addition, I was able to start learning my new job and supporting my new team five weeks earlier than they had anticipated. Over the next two months I continued to take initiative and create efficiency in my space, and my boss was taking notice. The efficiency I was creating was starting to have positive ripples throughout the team. I was only creating efficiency in my space, but because we worked as a team, any time my work was more efficient, I had created less waste in the team as a whole.

Most organizations are working toward their bottom line. Both the public and private sectors have limited budgets and required earnings, and no matter how much you hate how these things rule your life, they are what everyone is most concerned with. If you are able to improve the bottom line in whatever your position is, you will create a whole new worth for yourself within your organization.

Pillar 3: Adaptability

We are in an ever-changing world. Technology is moving faster than any of us can keep up. I don't know about you, but I still don't have the latest iPhone, computer, or smart car. Companies come and go like the change in my purse. Acquisitions and mergers make it impossible for some employees to know who they're actually working for. So much of our lives revolves around this constant evolution of technology that it makes it hard to keep up. Sometimes I don't even know why I have to do something, I just know I have to do it or the entire system breaks. Technology no longer revolves around us, we revolve around technology. Becoming adaptable to new situations and circumstances has become paramount in being seen as a leader. Organizations need people who can make good, quick decisions. If you think things are ever changing in your team, consider how much is shifting at the department and executive levels.

The biggest barrier to adaptability is emotion; fear being the most common one. When there are shifts in management or teams, your future can feel uncertain. Many large companies now have lay-offs every six months. In addition, many companies now have a large workforce of contractors, instead of full-time employees, meaning that full-time positions are being transitioned toward freelance and contract work more frequently. There is no certainty in today's workforce, and this is something that we must become unattached to. The fear of the unknown is scary; however, spending your time and energy focused on something so far out of your control is another way in which you may be working harder and not smarter. Focusing on your current requirements and ensuring they are hitting the target is the best way to prove you are irreplaceable by someone else.

Attachment to something or someone is another emotion often felt when things change. I had one client, we'll call her Mary for the purpose of the book, and Mary was a project manager. She had been hired to develop and manage a new HR program that would help teams throughout her organization become more empowered. Eight months into her project, her leadership realized that the program they had asked her to build was out of their perspective of the problems, not the problems people were actually encountering. Her entire program was dead in the water. For about two months she was irritable and frustrated at every new turn the project took, she felt like she had spent so much time working for nothing. She put in so many extra hours for deadlines, just to make sure everything was just right, and it was all for nothing, or so she thought. What she failed to see was that she was still employed! The false start was not blamed on her, yet she took it as her failure, and her managers began to see a shift in her work ethic and drive. Emotion can be a wonderful driving force, it is up to you to be able to recognize when it becomes a pulling force. Mary almost didn't catch it in time, she found out in her yearly review that those two months actually ended up costing her eight months of repair work with her leadership to get back to where she was prior to the reorganization of the project.

Fear and attachment are very common emotions around change. Our emotions are our responsibility. It is important to shift the negative emotions to positive ones. If you feel like you're going to bring a handicap to your team because of an emotion, step back, reflect on why you feel this way, accept that emotion, and find a way to shift it to a positive. This could take a few hours or a few days depending on how worked up you become, but don't let it take more than a week. The more you hold on to the negative, the more it will pull you deeper into the negative. Let change drive you, not pull you. Being agile and adaptable to change will also create less work for you. When emotion overcomes your work environment, that is time and effort you are spending on a feeling, instead of time and effort toward your work. Emotions don't seem like work, but when they are in a negative capacity they become draining, and working at a depleted capacity is a lot more work.

THE GOAL

I have mentioned several advantages to Smarter Not Harder. One of the greatest, however, is the ability to create more capacity. When you create efficiency in your work and your team, you are able to create greater capacity. This does not mean that you have to create more work for yourself or for your team. More capacity results in time for learning, apprenticeship, mentorship, or charity. It can also mean that because you've become more efficient you have time to revise and edit, and make your work even greater than the original. The goal is to create space for yourself to grow. Most organizations advertise learning and mentorships but not the time for them. Apprenticeships and mentorship fall directly into the Oprah. Working smarter allows you more capacity to work the other plays, and strategize your opportunities.

THE ALTER EGO

Sasha Fierce

There is a huge push in our culture to be "authentic." I can hear the "experts" of personal branding chime away: "Authenticity leads to success." "Authenticity is the key to attracting what you want in life." "Always bring your full self to work."

Authenticity is now a super-word within our culture. This argument suggests that everything we do should be rooted in our soul self, real and truthful. In a perfect world!

No one at the office wants to see your full self! If we brought our soul self to every situation in our lives, not only would we not be successful, we wouldn't be able to create the positive change we're looking to make. Your authentic self is not going to make you achieve greatness.

Powerful women understand this. Take Beyoncé, one of the most powerful women in our culture, she has an alter ego. Do you find this unauthentic? *Forbes* has named her one of America's Richest Self-Made Women multiple times. If you know anything about her story, you know that she admits to naturally being timid and very reserved, and yet she has made hundreds of millions for being a badass women's empowerment leader, and diva of all divas. She acknowledges she has an alter ego that comes out when she performs, and has even named her Sasha Fierce. Does this seem contradictory and hypocritical? Is she unauthentic? Of course not!

What so many people miss about the "authentic" movement is that you don't have just one authentic self. In an ideal world where we are all enlightened spiritual beings, one authentic self might prove to be divine, but we don't live in Utopia. It is appropriate and authentic to have multiple authentic selves. It all comes down to audience. How I talk to my husband is not how I talk to my boss. And how I talk to my boss is not how I talk to my mother. Just because I don't act or communicate the same way in different scenarios doesn't mean I'm not authentic, it simply means that I tailor myself to my audience.

Death Dealer

My family has a pretty good belly laugh every time they tell the story of when I told them I joined the army. I had been living in New York City working for a hedge fund when I decided to look into the military as an option for leadership growth. I decided to go one day during my lunch hour to the Times Square Recruiting Station and take a look at what options there were. The Times Square Recruiting Station is a little square building made of glass walls that sits, literally, in the center of Times Square. I walked through the door with my high-waisted pencil skirt, silk blouse, and pumps, and was greeted with wide eyes and looks of confusion. "Excuse me miss, are you lost?" Several men, all wearing a different uniform, peered around their cubicle walls as I stood there at the doorway. Confidently I said, "I'm interested in talking with an army recruiter about what opportunities the army has for professionals." They all looked around like they were being punked, looking for the hidden cameras and waiting on Ashton Kutcher to storm through the door. After a few seconds the army recruiter walked toward me, shook my hand, introduced himself, and walked me toward his desk. It took several appointments, tests, and physicals before I was accepted into the army's Officer Candidate School. I had been accepted just before Thanksgiving. I went home to Missouri for a weekend to tell my family I was changing my career path. My mother, sister, and step-father were all in the kitchen chatting when I decided it was time to tell them. I stepped through the kitchen doorway, and onto the tile. As I was nervous for their reaction, I twirled my hair and did a little nervous toe sweep with one foot. Unplanned, I did one full ballet twirl with my swept foot, not wanting to look them in the eye as I told them, "So, I think I'm going to join the army."

Laughter took over the house. I had just done a ballet twirl as I told them I was joining the army during a time of war. My sister, under her laughter and with a squeal said, "You're going to die!"

Safe to say, my goofy, girly personality wasn't quite going to work for the task ahead. I had accidentally become a barrier breaker to women in combat roles, and in this role "being me" wasn't quite going to make me successful, or make the impact that needed to be made for future generations of women in the army. The barriers that myself, and others, were attempting to break had large stakes and required a larger game than most. I gave up two things in the aspiration for women to unequivocally serve in combat roles. I gave up my femininity and put my personal life on hold. We have not yet reached the level of *Starship Troopers*, where men and women serve equally; the military was and is still working through the effects of women in combat roles, and we were up against political and social landscape. My example is one that is in the extreme, because it was occurring at a time of war and in a war zone. I do not suggest you taking any of the measures I did. No one told me to do these things, but it was a decision I made to ensure others developed a certain perception about me. The perception of me being single and available was one I didn't want my all male soldiers to have. I deliberately wore a uniform one size too big so my figure didn't show, and I changed my feminine body language into a broad shouldered demeanor. I know many women in my situation who didn't make these deliberate decisions, they had their own way of approaching it, but for that time I adapted my persona for my audience, an audience of all male soldiers.

When I finished up my leadership time, I was asked to work for the Special Forces Task Force I had worked with on several missions. I was one of the few women who had front line combat experience, and further a graduate degree in sustainable development, which was at that time an element of the Special Forces Mission. I had done several route clearance missions for this unit during my platoon leader time. I had a reputation for being professional and a go-getter. When I began working on projects for them and briefing high-level officers, I gained the nickname Death Dealer. It came two-fold, one I looked like death coming to work for them after a year in country (my job was to find roadside bombs, so it had taken a little bit of a toll on me at that point), and two I had a no bulls*** mentality that resulted in the "I can kill you with one look" look. This unit was the best of the best and to be taken seriously. I had to ensure they knew I was serious about my job, about the mission, and about my outcomes. The side-eye of death is the look I would give when anyone tried to take advantage of or leverage my level of experience or gender against me. I was authentic to myself, I was not doing anything that I deemed untruthful or fake, I simply tailored my persona to my audience.

The New World

Before I had joined the army I had never used swear words, but I learned very quickly in a culture predominantly of young twenty-something males that swearing was "emphasis." If I swore it was not to offend, it was to emphasize to a specific audience; it was part of the culture I was in. When I left the army and went back into the corporate sector my hard ass, Ice Princess, Death Dealer personas were no longer the work personas that were going to make me successful. I worked for a Fortune 100 high-tech company where the personality was passive, calm, and collected. I had to quickly learn to turn off my potty mouth. For a lot of people swearing is considered profanity, offensive, and disrespectful. I had to learn to emphasize in a different way when I re-entered the corporate workforce.

When I re-entered corporate, it became very apparent very quickly that I was no longer working with one type of person. In the military I generalized my audience and didn't focus on personalities as much as I focused on gender. Remember, I had an "us vs. them" mentality. They all seemed way similar to each other and it was an easy grouping from my perspective, we were all trained to be a very similar type of soldier. In corporate, no such training and dominant culture exist. I began to see independent personality types much more clearly, and began to see how differently personality types communicated.

Understanding your audience is so important to your success. Being able to tailor your communication to your audience is the epitome of professionalism. Catering your communication to your audience also plays into the Smarter, Not Harder. It may seem like a task in the learning stage, but once you become skillful you'll see that you spend less time explaining things because your person gets it on the first time. Becoming skillful in communication doesn't take away from your authentic self, it expands it.

Likability Factor

One thing to always keep in mind is that if people don't like you, they will work with you because they have to, but you may not always get the best out of them. For people to want to work with you and be enthusiastic about working with you, they have to like you. Now, this does not mean that everyone will like you or you should cater to each person's every need, it just means that you need to understand how and why people perceive you the way they do and why they feel about you the way they do. If your likability is due to something you're doing or not doing in general, like you're always late for work or you're disorganized, then you can adjust. If it is because of them and their bias, and they think that a general smile is flirting, then effective communication around your intention will help mediate the different points of view.

Remember my story of Ice Princess from earlier? What I didn't mention then is that while I was in one of the hardest basic officer courses in the army I was also writing my thesis for my master's degree. Where most of my classmates had engineering degrees and easily understood the material, I was coming from a political science background and found the material to be very intensive and difficult. In addition to struggling through the course, I was also the only one out of 65 students who was working through a graduate degree. While I had finished my master's coursework when I entered the army, I still had to research and write my thesis. Because I joined during a time of war, when we were engaged in two theaters, I knew that if I didn't finish my thesis during this period, it would be years before I'd be able to get back to it. So while my classmates went out for drinks after and socialized, I was studying and writing until midnight, only to wake up at 4 a.m. the next day to do it all over again. When they used to mess around and take their time getting to dismissal formation, I was eagerly and impatiently waiting, knowing that I had double the work to get to.

When I took over in my leadership role of the class, I did not change anything to what had been done the past several months by my classmates. The difference was that I didn't have time for horse play or socializing. This was perceived as my being cold and abrupt, instead of being dedicated and motivated. What it took me several years to understand was that if you aren't likable, you won't be successful. There has to be a likability factor about you to be promotable. For you to be a leader, you have to know how to effectively communicate in a way that your team can digest it. I did not have the likability factor in my scenario. While people respected that I worked hard, I did not get good peer evaluations, which impact your class ranking, because I was not likable.

One of my clients for years had issues with her manager. She was a branch manager within a regional bank. She came with a decade of expertise in banking management and policy management. Her branch became the most successful branch, bringing in more profits than any other branch manager; yet, when it came to her professional relationship with the regional manager, their relationship was strained unlike the other managers across the company. She was never invited to manager breakfasts or invited for one-on-one lunches. She felt like there was a good ol' boys club happening, but didn't understand why another woman manager was there if it was a good ol' boys club. The regional bank was a center point for a larger community, and because she didn't fit in with the company community, she wasn't accepted into the larger city community. Her ability to be successful in the city and be involved in community leadership positions meant she had to fix the relationship with the regional manager. After a year of "dealing" with and trying to understand the strain on their relationship, she was in a meeting with him when he mentioned that she was entitled and her grossly substantial salary meant that he didn't have to deal with her, she could do it on her own.

The strain she was feeling and lack of likability from this regional manager was due to her making more than him. She had been hired several years before the company was re-organized and a new structure was instituted, including her boss' position; her salary was grandfathered into the negotiation. She had to read into the situation, and realized that he felt that as a regional manager he should be the highest earner, not a branch head, even if her qualifications and education justified the salary. Now that she understood his underlying issue had nothing to do with her, and all to do with his issue of her making more, the problem wasn't what she assumed it to be. We spent the next year working to build out their relationship. Her larger goal was to be a community leader, and that required a better relationship with her regional manager.

Using the One-on-One play, she began to genuinely get to know him. Instead of waiting for invitations, she initiated encounters. Her goal was to understand his point of view and personality so she could leverage that against her future encounters with him. She began to involve him, and ask for his presence at the branch when she initiated a new efficiency plan (the Smarter, Not Harder). And she began to leverage the other branch managers, again using the One-on-One play to create a better relationship, and create influence amongst the larger manager team (the Oprah). Not everything worked, and it took a lot of initiative and continued effort to make positive strides; but she became part of the larger company community, and further became involved in community boards from her connections.

THE GOAL

As you move through the playbook and start to understand each play you will at some point likely feel confused, like there are conflicting plays of the game.

"I'm supposed to care about how people perceive me."

"I'm supposed to be concerned with how people perceive me due to their bias and not my doing."

"I shouldn't care if everyone likes me."

"I need to work on being likable."

And you're absolutely right, it can be confusing. The key to your work persona is balance, it is all about knowing who your audience is and tailoring how you communicate and work with them to best set yourself up for success. Human nature, personality differences, perception, and bias will always be a factor in your success. How you react, leverage, and take action toward these factors will be the key to your sanity when you feel like you're up against a brick wall.

THE KATNISS

When you think of Katniss from *The Hunger Games* what comes to mind? A risk taker? A skilled archer? A girl who fights for herself and others? I named this play the Katniss because it is all about confidence. Not just about having it, but creating it when you don't have it. Katniss wasn't always confident and wasn't the first one out the door, but she knew she had to create it, or there would be dire consequences.

If you're thinking, I'm confident, and I'm pretty sure I embrace it; I want to challenge you. When was the last time you second-guessed a decision because you didn't think anyone else would agree? When was the last time you let someone talk over you in a meeting because you thought it'd be rude to interrupt? When was the last time you stopped yourself from asking for a raise, because you thought they'd give it to you when they thought you were ready?

We have been taught that confidence is ego, and that it is not a positive quality in a woman. In our personal lives we're told that men like confident women, but soon find out that you can't be too confident. You have no idea where the balance is. One relationship book says one thing, another one says another. While working through the Katniss I want you to erase this notion of being confident so someone likes you or is attracted to you. Confidence has nothing to do with anyone else, and everything to do with you. I will say it again: confidence has nothing to do with anyone else. Confidence is solely for you and on your terms. In this play I will walk through how to shut down the doubt game, uncover the missing pieces to confidence, work through feeling like you're in over your head, and taking risks. This play is designed for you to rid yourself of the self-sabotaging behaviors that are preventing you from reaching your full potential in your career. To go further and have greater success, others must see your hunger and drive to succeed in the midst of hurdles and obstacles. Leaders must be able to control out-of-control situations and be able to tackle the hard decisions; you must be able to show your tenacity and dedication in your responsibilities to be seen as a leader.

Shut Out The Doubt Game

Dr. Karyl McBride conducted a study on women. She discovered that "a significant portion of strong, independent, high achieving women who have good self-esteem, can still be plagued by self-doubt." I am one of these women. I have self-doubt thoughts, I used to have a lot more. It starts out as a simple internal thought, that begins to grow, and grow, and spiderweb out of control. Your initial little tiny doubt quickly turns into a dinosaur that is hard to wrangle.

According to the Laboratory of Neuro Imaging at the University of Southern California, the average person has 70,000 thoughts per day. Of those 70,000 thoughts, their results found that about 98 percent of the thoughts were the same. This means that the majority of our time is spent thinking the same thing over and over again. This is why you hear experts say your thoughts define you. But how do you change your thoughts? They change over time, but you've been thinking the same way for the past 20+ years.

I'm a believer in making change a game. If it isn't fun, it won't last. The game I've built around self-doubt involves one simple question, "Would a man think this?" The goal isn't to compare yourself against men, it isn't about anyone else. The goal is to identify your thoughts, and gain control of them. Growing quantitative evidence shows that women tend to have more self-doubt than men. If this is natural, there's no need to get upset by the statistics, use them for your benefit. Asking myself "would a man think this," when my thoughts start to spiderweb has become a powerful tool for shutting down self-doubt. In most cases it makes me realize how silly most of my self-doubt thoughts are. It is difficult to re-wire how you think, the intent with this question is to start identifying self doubt thoughts, and shut them off closer and closer to the initial thought, before they spider web out of control.

I have one client who is the type of woman I explained above: she is independent, has high self-esteem, and is a successful mid-level sales manager. She had quit her previous job as a sales director to do some traveling. Upon her return she was asked to interview for a company she had previously interviewed for, but didn't get the position. She liked the company. She thought the reason she didn't get the position last time was because they had already had someone in mind, and she was interviewed for a future position. The interview went great, the manager really liked the experience she'd bring to the team. This was a sales support position, a few steps lower than the sales director/manager positions she'd held in the past. She was told the pay would be lower than her last job (as a sales manager), and quite a bit lower than her previous job (as a sales director), as she would have fewer responsibilities in this role. The hiring manager called around to her references and she received glowing accolades. When the offer letter came in, it came in $5,000 less than her previous job, which she was prepared for. She has always been told to counter the offer though, so she emailed me her counter-offer email and asked for advice. I love this client, she is so fun, enthusiastic, and positivity exudes from her 100% of the time. Her counter-offer letter was awful though. In her email, her personality outshined her professionalism. In her request for a higher offer, she had a lot of fluff, and spunk, asked multiple times, almost to the state of begging. I helped her begrudgingly re-write her email without the fluff and most of the personality, and made it direct and to the point of what her counter-offer was and why.

Over the next three days she would text me saying she thought she made a mistake with the counter-offer. She didn't think they'd have the money in the department to increase the offer. She was worried they weren't even going to respond. For three days, the silence increased the self-doubt. I kept reminding her that in a large corporation like this one, it takes time for things to get approved. On the fourth day she texted me with complete shock, she finally received a counter-offer... and it was for $5,000 more than her counter. Her counter had convinced them she was worth more than their initial offer, more than her counter-offer. Even if her responsibilities were fewer than her last position, they knew they were getting a rockstar and wanted to make sure she'd come onto their team with excitement and eagerness.

I kept asking her in all of her times of self-doubt, "Would a man think this?" When she was doubting the pay she was asking for, when she was doubting they'd write her back, when she was doubting she was worth the extra work on their part. She hated me at first. "I don't want to think like a man, I want to think like me." "I don't want to think like anyone else." I had to remind her that this is a game, not to make her think like a man, but to help her recognize the self-sabotaging nature of her self-doubt.

Are You In Over Your Head

Feeling like you're in over your head is a common feeling. Whether you're starting a new job, going back to school, or becoming a mother for the first time, change can feel overwhelming. The feeling of being overwhelmed can make us feel like we're unworthy of the great things happening to us. We must again start to recognize these thoughts of self-doubt. I use the same trick as before but change the verb, "Would a man believe this?"

I had a client who had switched professions about five years into her career. She went from working in advertising to working in high-tech sales. She was excited for the career change realizing advertising wasn't for her, but terrified that she had made a huge mistake. In her interview she connected really well with the hiring manager regarding her client relationship skills from advertising, and she knew that was a large reason she got the job. But when the offer negotiation was complete, and she stepped outside of the initial excitement, she started to panic. She didn't know anything about the thing she was going to be selling. She wasn't that knowledgeable on her iPhone, much less a complex routing system. She called me with a list of concerns and hesitation regarding the new job. "Should she call them and tell them she decided not to take it?" "Should she get into something more similar, like marketing?" My response to her was, "Would a man question his ability to learn something new? Are you capable of learning?" That is all that was standing in her way: learning. In all of her fears and doubts about not knowing the job, she was simply going to have to learn.

It is easy to let these thoughts spiral out of control and become larger than they should ever be. It is up to you to catch yourself in the act of overthinking. I am one of the biggest culprits of overthinking, and constantly have to overcome this trait and habit by becoming conscientious and cognizant of my thoughts. It is going to be nearly impossible to try and rid yourself of self-doubt in a few months or even years when it comes from an entire lifetime of conditioning. What you are doing with this question is changing the internal dialogue and conversation when it creeps up.

Risky Business

I've given you the game to smash self-doubt, now it's time to take it one notch further. To be a Katniss in the Bold Maneuver you must learn to not only take risks, but love taking risks. Katniss objects to the status-quo. With the status-quo there is no growth or learning. When you're working through the Bold Maneuver you are going to be trying new things, and you will never get it right on the first play. In the event that you do get it right the first time, one play may work in one situation but not in another, or it will work with one person but not with another. The best lessons for growth are failures, and you're reading this book for professional growth. But Katniss isn't afraid of failure, she goes all in. Risk taking and failure go hand in hand. Nothing was ever done successfully on the first try. No matter how big or how small, there is always a failure in the path of success. Trial and error is part of the fun in building out new skills. You become a researcher in your own life. You create a hypothesis for how you think something will work, implement the play, and see if it worked out the way you thought it would.

Implementing the Katniss at your work means that you start taking small calculated risks in an attempt to achieve greater results. I don't want you to go big or go home. If you take too big of a risk too early out of the gate, you may be sent home for good. The kind of risks I want you to take are attempting different methods of getting to know someone, different methods to create efficiency in your work, or building your skills to negotiate. I know you are intelligent and successful in your own right, but I don't want you to take a risk in the first few months that could jeopardize your employment.

THE GOAL

What a lot of people try to do to be taken seriously or show confidence is inadvertently create a douchey persona because they focus on attention grabbing characteristics that they think will "make" the other person listen to them, swearing, nonchalant demeanor, aggressive tactics. In the Bold Maneuver, the Katniss is about you and no one else. Creating confidence when you're feeling unsure, embracing your confidence when you think it's a disadvantage to your goal. The Katniss will be one of your most played plays in the Bold Maneuver. To play the other plays you will have to consistently shut down the internal thoughts of self-doubt. This play requires dedication, consistency, and self-awareness. I want you to start to catch your internal dialogue, change the conversation, and be the Katniss you're supposed to be. Start to recognize when you follow your gut instinct instead of shying away from it, and create the confidence you've always wanted through action. Confidence can be infectious if it's genuine. Creating confidence in yourself can permeate through your team.

You and your team will be more involved and interested in solving problems that inadvertently can achieve better results. If you and your team are too timid to make mistakes, fewer problems will be addressed. Results are what your leaders are looking for in their business, and what will determine if they promote you or keep you where you are.

THE ICE PRINCESS

"Do what you feel in your heart to be right—for you'll be criticized anyway. You'll be damned if you do, and damned if you don't."

– Eleanor Roosevelt

o you often feel like you're being judged or stereotyped? Does the fear of being labeled keep you from going after what you want or taking risks in a positive direction? Maybe this is a childhood trauma that has caused you to be cautious about how people perceive you. Maybe you've subconsciously shut yourself off from work relationships because you've had negative experiences with being open in the past.

Fear of what others think about us is a much greater hindrance than most realize. Fear is a very real roadblock to success that isn't always so visible to us. There are many reasons that fear may be showing up for you, I find that with most of my clients it has to do with the fear of misperception. Are there any instances you can think of where you let your fear of being labeled prevent you from doing something, then weeks or months later wished had you taken the initiative?

You've been working the same way for 20+ years, it can be hard adjusting your approach. That is why it is called the Bold Maneuver; it is moving you beyond your natural approach in taking action. You may be getting results, but if you picked up this book, you want exceptional and uncommon results.

I made the Ice Princess the last play of the Bold Maneuver because it is the hardest play to achieve. While it is very much achievable, it is one that requires a more consistent intent and mental reminders. We use the other plays in the playbook as leveraging points to execute the Bold Maneuver; in this play, it is important to keep the other plays in play, while simultaneously letting go of your fear of being labeled, being wrong, and being criticized. So much of why you're not finding the success you want is because you're afraid of what others will think if you do this or do that.

I Just Want Everyone To Like Me

One thing I wish I could change about myself is my emotional need for everyone to like me. This is different from the Likability Factor. This is about an aching need to be liked by everyone. Our reality tends to be shifty based on this deep-rooted childhood yearning to be liked. We tend to be overly in our heads, analyzing every encounter, hoping we did and said the right thing so he/she will like us. I've had a few therapy sessions, even tried hypnosis to help me rid this silly notion from my personality, but I've come to terms with the fact that, the "I want to be liked" inner child will always be with me. She is a decade's worth of habit. We all have childhood idiosyncrasies that follow us into adulthood; sometimes they stay with us for just a few years until we substitute them with new habits, and sometimes they stay with us our entire lives. I still have this inner child that wants to be liked, but any time it overtakes my thoughts and creates fear and doubt, I am more able to talk her down quickly and easily.

Whether or not you have this same need, you likely still find yourself initially upset when you find out that someone doesn't like you. I know that we try to brush it off, and it usually goes something like: "I don't care what they think." "Screw it! It's not my problem." But underneath those words is an inner dialogue about what you could have done differently or could do differently to make them like you. The way to make it past this desire is to catch this inner dialogue as it is occurring and come to center with the following.

People will find reasons not to like you. Race and gender are the easy targets. Scientists at Royal Holloway University found that we naturally tend to be attracted to people who look like us because our brain perceives the similarity as more trustworthy. There are many conscious and subconscious reasons why someone may not like you. We may feel, and in reality, be the victim of racism or genderism, but we must not become victims of their perception. When we feel victimized, we begin to use emotion to counter their judgment. It is your personal responsibility to recognize when you start to feel victimized, accept the feeling, and create a new internal dialogue where your confidence in self outplays the demeaning noise of other people.

Judgy Judgerson

No matter what you do, you're not nice enough, not bold enough, not dainty enough, not direct enough, not a*** enough. You can't win! The struggle is real! How are you supposed to get things done and prove your worth if you're always perceived as too this or too that? Perception is one of those things we've learned to hate, that we need to learn to leverage.

Have you ever not liked anyone just because? Maybe you felt something was off with them. Maybe the first impression rubbed you the wrong way. We all find reasons not to like someone. If you're reading this thinking that you are above the instant judgement, then you are a better person than I. No matter how much I try to keep an open mind, an open heart, and be empathetic toward others, I can catch myself every now and then being super critical and judgy. This is natural human behavior that in many cases stems from our cognitive biases. We reason, evaluate, remember, and associate someone or something based our own preferences and beliefs regardless of if there is information to the contrary. Our preferences and beliefs shape our perceptions far more than we would ever like to believe. We are shaped by our life experiences, big and small, good and bad, and all of us make choices from our interpretation of our experiences.

Understanding cognitive bias is an important tool for a multitude of reasons. For the purpose of the Bold Maneuver, it helps you recognize that everyone you meet, everyone you know, comes to the table with bias first. The recognition of cognitive bias when dealing with other people will help you approach people with empathy. Even when you catch yourself in your own mental thought web of bias, you will be able to recognize it, and accept its presence, and begin to experience the moment with openness. Once you recognize cognitive bias happening, you will begin to feel less attached to someone's perception of you. In many cases someone's perception of you has less to do with you and more to do with them.

When I was a platoon leader in the army, I was deployed to Afghanistan. My job was to lead a forty-man team of engineers to clear roads of roadside bombs. I became one of the less than one percent of women serving in the military to lead combat operations. At a time when we weren't even "technically" allowed to be in front-line combat roles, a few of us were already there. I was about a month into my role when my teammate, my equal in the enlisted ranks, the platoon sergeant, pulled me aside. In a small supply room with another soldier he began to berate me for my unprofessionalism. "You better stop it! I can't believe you are so naive! All your laughing and smiling around the soldiers... anyone who sees you will think you're a flirt!" I couldn't believe this encounter. For years, this memory dug at me. Was I in the wrong? Was I not allowed to have a personality because I was a woman in this role? How could I be naive, how could he be naive? We were running twelve- to fourteen-hour missions six days a week, doing one of the most unpopular jobs of the war. Was I not allowed to bond with my soldiers? Not allowed to create an environment of camaraderie, when the stress of the mission is more than many can handle? All because I'm a woman? I know I wasn't unprofessional, but maybe being one of the barrier breakers to this field I was held to a different standard. To this day, this memory irks me. I have to remind myself that he was angry due to his bias, not due to my behavior. I was good at my job, I always held a professional demeanor, and I took my role very seriously. In the months following this encounter, I thought that everyone else had to have seen what he did. It was my fault for wearing a smile. I made decisions and acted based on this, based on his bias, and I will forever regret that I let his bias determine my outlook.

How many times have you let someone's perception or bias of you infect your mind into thinking it is you, and everyone else must see the same thing? You must start to catch yourself in these in-thought moments, catch them and release. Everyone is working off a bias, not everyone sees what that person sees, and you're probably making a bigger deal out of it than it really is. Once you recognize that the issue in front of you is perception and bias, you can start to work through why they see you in this way. This is when you leverage your One-on-One play to outmaneuver their bias. This is a ninja move that requires a shift from emotion to logic and assumption to investigation. If you're able to transfer the negativity of a situation into a positive diagnostic you will create a space for learning and remove the space for loathing.

THE GOAL

We are all labeled. No matter who you are or where you're from, you are going to be labeled. In the previous plays you've learned to be self-aware and in tune to your surroundings and the people around you, and the importance behind these skills. The Ice Princess play takes a bit of a different approach. Some of your most self-sabotaging behavior is out of fear. Take the confidence you gained from the Katniss and begin to let go of the self-doubt and fear that is hindering your forward momentum. It is important to recognize if you are creating more fear by being more aware. I want you to be able to leverage the information you've gained through initiating the plays for your advantage, but it will not work if you're in a constant state of anxiety. You will make mistakes no matter how well intended your actions are, and you will make mistakes in applying the Bold Maneuver, but the most important thing is not to beat yourself up about it but learn from it. Your fear is getting in the way of you leveraging the lessons and determining and executing your next move. In the Katniss you learned the traits of failing forward and resiliency. They come into play here, for when you do fail, are wrong, or could have done better, you must reflect, learn, be proud of the try, and move forward.

It is up to you to create the life you want, the change you want, and the success you want, but it is going to be mission impossible if you're fearful of every move you make.

FUNCTIONAL FITNESS

"When you are tough on yourself, life is going to be infinitely easier on you."

– Zig Ziglar

T here is a small majority of people who are prepared for boot camp when they sign on the dotted line to join the military. Some may have trained for the physical aspect, but very few are prepared mentally and emotionally for the challenges that come with it. This is because the program is designed to break the soldier mentally, emotionally, and physically. When the bus full of recruits first pulls in at the barracks everything you thought you knew is turned upside down. If you have confidence, it will be broken. If you have opinions, those will be thrown out. If you are competent, you will be proven otherwise. If you are logical, you will find yourself becoming emotional. Each recruit comes in with different strengths and weakness, and the job of the drill sergeants is to break each recruit mentally, emotionally, and physically. This may seem counterproductive to someone looking at this situation from the outside in, but there is a very important reason each recruit is meant to be broken. Recruits enter boot camp as non-combatants, but they must leave as warriors.

Boot camp is in many ways a resiliency program. The end product is a soldier who is prepared for dire circumstances he/she may encounter. Most people aren't inherently built this way though, we aren't prepared to react in terrible life or death situations. The entire program is built to instill discipline, confidence, and fortitude, so they are capable of achieving feats they view as impossible. To build these three elements they create calculated situations where disarray, failure, and fear develop within the recruits. Discipline, confidence, and fortitude are learned through adversity and therefore can only be taught in uncomfortable situations when the recruit is unprepared and confused.

The military is historically one of the best trainers in resiliency and perseverance, and this is because it conditions these traits within its organizations. Functional fitness is becoming more mentally, emotionally, and physically fit so you are seen as an exceptional contender for growth and leadership. Just as the military prepares its recruits for leadership in this capacity, so must you.

Functional fitness is the foundation for the Bold Maneuver. Executing the Bold Maneuver with an unstable foundation will result in a much longer journey because you will have to consistently back off the plays to reinforce the foundation. When doing any kind of exercise, stable footing is a much better starting point than quicksand. The same goes for the Bold Maneuver, to achieve greater success and go further, you will achieve much stronger results with a strong foundation. I've put functional fitness as the last move in the Bold Maneuver because it is one move you'll want to practice continuously, regardless of where you are in your bold maneuver. Functional fitness is the conditioning you need to have in place for all of the other plays to run smoothly; if you're not taking care of your mind and body you're not going to clearly see when you need to use one play over another.

Remember my three rules from before?

1. S*** Happens
2. Life's Not Fair
3. No One Owes You Anything

Sometimes things just do not go the way you thought they would or should. You did everything right, but now you've been thrown a curve ball, and you feel like your life is out of your control. So often people want to escape the struggles, but if you do, you will miss the most influential lessons that are capable of propelling you forward. If you are able to condition yourself mentally, emotionally, and physically for these circumstances, the struggle will seem insignificant to the opportunities. People who use adversity as a driving force are able to step back from the situation, reflect, learn, and react.

As much as you don't want to admit it, your mental, emotional, and physical state affects your ability to do your job well. Companies, whether they are legally or ethically permitted to do so, promote employees who have their stuff together. They want someone who exudes clarity and class, someone who is logical, cool, calm, and collected, and someone who looks like success. You may see these things as irrelevant to your abilities and your competence, but if I turn the story around, does it change your point of view?

When you are looking for your partner, do you look for someone who is scatterbrained, maybe aloof? What's more attractive than irrational and temperamental? How about someone who is sick and on the verge of diabetes?

I'm guessing these qualities do not make up your ideal partner in life. Unfortunately, these are not the ideal qualities businesses are looking for in partners either. This may seem like a cruel parallel or unfair analogy, and it isn't always the case, but the reality of how you look for a partner is very similar to how a company looks for its leaders. I'm not trying to make you perfect, that is an impossible feat, my goal is to help you become more self-aware so that when you start to veer off, as we all do, you can more easily get back on track without having to start again.

Much like in sports where some people are just naturally gifted athletes, so is true for mental, emotional, and physical fitness. Some people are naturally more self-aware, emotionally aware, and fit. Those of us who weren't naturally gifted those traits must practice them to become good at them.

Mental Fitness

If you could have lunch with one of the most influential people on the *Time's* list, who would it be? If you need to take a moment to look up the list, I want you to do so. I want you to ask them the following questions in your head, and then I want you to answer it.

What is the key to success?

(Answer)

Is making it to the top easier or harder than you thought?

(Answer)

At what level were you able to make the impact you always dreamt of making?

(Answer)

Was your answer to the key to success luck? So much of what pop culture tries to impart on us is that success is driven by luck. Being in the right place at the right time. I doubt that many of those successful enough to make the *Time's* Most Influential List would say they became successful through luck. I bet the majority of the answers are much more complex. They'd likely include a story or two of the struggles that catapulted them to their success. And they'd probably mention a few key people who influenced and empowered them to push through adversity.

I bet that there is an outlier or two that would say luck. I also bet that luck is their answer because they are not yet ready to share their full story. Luck has become a popular success story within pop culture because as a society we prefer to omit that the world can be difficult and dirty. But very few of the top successful stories would admit that their success was by chance alone. A lot of time luck is looked at as the result of setting the right conditions, but that isn't luck at all. An easy example of this is *Disney* child stars. We may see easy and lucky, but that isn't the real success story. The success story looks something more like, music lessons from the age of two, auditions every weekend instead of playing outside. Hundreds of nos and rejections in-between the few yeses. We like to see luck because that is the more glamorous story than the real one. The real story is they set the conditions through effort to be in the right place at the right time.

When you answered whether it was easier or harder to get to the top, did you answer easier? I bet instinctively you actually answered harder. This is because subconsciously you know that being the best at something is much harder than it looks. We must bring that subconscious understanding to the surface so that when you're up against a wall, you don't internalize it as an issue, you immediately begin to strategize its removal.

Your goals may not include making it to the executive level, CEO, or board of directors, but I have a feeling you see yourself leading and becoming a change maker within your organization or field. You likely chose the field you did because you want to make a difference. More impact means more influence. That doesn't necessarily mean that higher position equals more influence, but I bet their answer reflects decades of work, of which they wouldn't have been able to reach had they not pushed through all of the roadblocks in their path.

As I mentioned in the beginning of this book, when it comes to high achieving women, up to 90 percent choose to leave their field because of work place problems. I have no details of their issues and problems and in no capacity want to suggest that their leaving wasn't valid or merited, I just want you to reflect on how large that number is. If women continue to leave in this capacity, the issues that we wish to see changed will likely never occur. No one is going to fight our fights for us. Whether the issue is solely in your court or encompasses a larger group, you are responsible for the future you envision and mental fitness is about conditioning yourself mentally for challenges you'll face in achieving your vision.

Emotional Fitness

In the Ice Princess play I spoke about cognitive bias and how people will not like you due to their own perception and biases. If words like "drama queen," "basket case," "emotional," and "irrational" get thrown around any time you show an inkling of emotion, that is because the person on the other end of the emotion is uncomfortable with being on the receiving end. In some cases it is another person throwing out words to make the person on the other end of your conversation feel empowered. In most cases it is less about you and your "issues" and more about them and theirs. In cases like this, you must simply ignore their immediate reaction that often comes by way of labeling you, and move on. This example is not what we're focused on in emotional fitness. We all show and carry emotion, I have no intent on making you a robot or the epitome of perfection. If you haven't recognized it yet, I'm all about real; and having emotions is real.

Emotional fitness is the ability to recognize your emotions, understand where the emotion is coming from, acknowledge them for what they are, and manage them for the situation. What are the emotions that come to mind with the following examples?

Your co-workers continue to cut you off when you're briefing in a meeting.

Your boss made a condescending comment to you in front of your co-workers.

You worked for weeks on a project that is now being put aside.

Self-awareness comes more easily to some than to others, but we must build the skill of recognizing our states of emotion. One of the most common emotions in the work environment is defensiveness. We are putting everything we have into our work, and when someone doubts us or questions our outcomes we can take their reaction personally against ourselves and our abilities. People like to say that they're justified in being defensive because they traded their time for their work: time with their family, time doing the things they love. My response to this is: they were compensated for that time. The best trick to curbing emotions when we recognize them is accepting the change and being able to quickly adjust and adapt to the new situation, pillar three in the Smarter, Not Harder.

Have you ever had a boss or a co-worker who was always just super cool, calm, and collected no matter what the situation was? I don't know about you, but I always looked up to these people. I was mesmerized by this ability because, between you and me, I can have a hot temper. What I've learned over the years in managing emotion is the emotion is in most every case driven by ego. And so to manage emotion, I have to first manage my ego. I know what you're thinking already, "but guys have huge egos and they don't have to manage them." But remember, we're not trying to be a man, we're trying to beat them at their own game. If you feel like your work is not being taken seriously, your project importance is being downplayed, taking away the ego of why you believe this can allow you to focus on the plays that can help you counter the issues. It all comes back to the strategy and playing the plays to create leverage. The goal is to become conditioned to catching your emotions when they begin to emerge, reflecting and understanding why you're feeling the way you do, and reacting with one of the plays, leveraging the situation for your benefit.

Physical Fitness

I said something terrible at the beginning of this chapter, that physicality matters. Please do not take this as me saying you have to look like a Victoria's Secret model to be successful, or if you are unique in your appearance you will never get ahead. I do not believe that, and I hope you do not either. Being physically fit has more to do with your mental and emotional state, than it does your physical state. The goal is not to be a size zero and starving. The goal is to have an outlet for your mental and emotional energy. An outlet that pushes you and challenges you, at the physical, mental, and emotional levels. An outlet where you feel safe to fail and grow. An outlet where you recognize and actualize your power. Functional fitness is not about becoming the perfect specimen of a human, it is about real body conditioning for the real world. Companies want people who are conditioned to try, to take calculated risks, to be uncomfortable, and fail gracefully. Conditioning yourself for physical functional fitness creates a safe outlet for you to develop these skills. Physical functional fitness can look very differently. It could be yoga, running, weight training, cross fit, anything that helps push you past what you think your limits are.

One of my favorite activities is obstacle courses. Have you ever done one? Man, they are hard! You come away scratched up, beat up, and emotionally and physically exhausted. They have become very popular over the last few years, and I find that either most people have done one or have one on their bucket list. I use the example of the military in this chapter because they have nearly perfected the ability to push people past their fears, and obstacle courses are one of their go-to methods. Whether your fear is trusting others, not having the experience, feeling unprepared, or not feeling comfortable in new situations; obstacle courses provide mental, emotional, and physical obstacles to overcome. The end state of an obstacle course is to show you that you are stronger than you think you are. Whether you completed every obstacle or just a few, you walk away having a new appreciation for your abilities, an appreciation that was created by struggle and adversity. You are required to face your fears, push through them, and conquer them.

For me, physical functional fitness is one exercise, the pull-up. The pull-up is looked at as an exercise that women aren't capable of doing, we just simply don't have the upper body strength for it. In my four years in the army, I was never able to do even one. And in the years after the army, I always tried to build them into my workouts, but was still never able to do one. While it was always a bucket list item I never judged myself for not being able to do them, I just wished I could. On my last deployment to Afghanistan, there was a pull-up bar outside the dining facility. As everyone entered, you had to do five pull-ups. Now, let me just say that it wasn't required for civilians, but I still had this want to do them. It took me a month of lifting and practicing to just be able to do one. For another month, I was at one and a half. But every day I had a goal of doing 20. That could be one at a time, or in multiples, whatever my body could do, I would do 20. Before you know it, I could do five at a time. Now I have always been a fairly confident individual. I tend to be way harder on myself than anyone else, but I'd say I'm confident. When I was able to do all five pull-ups before entering the dining facility as soldiers and marines lined up, my confidence in myself shot up even more. I had accomplished something I never had before, I had done something that "women aren't able to do." This confidence not only improved my physical performance, but it made me more determined and confident in my work. Pushing past this lifelong goal created an inner strength that started to show up in all areas of my life. This is the true end state of physical fitness. Not the skinny jeans or the looking good, but the inner conditioning for confidence and strength.

THE GOAL

Functional fitness is a bit different from the plays, yet it has similar contributions to achieving the Bold Maneuver. The six plays are actions that create leverage points... functional fitness is a state of being. All require practice, success and failure, learning and reflecting to become efficient. Being conditioned is having a consistent pattern of behavior or thought as a result of being subjected to circumstances or situations. When you encounter unfair situations at work, or struggle with personalities, being in a state of functional fitness can allow you to more easily approach the situation, react in a manner that you are able to quickly choose the appropriate play to leverage the situation for the positive.

OPPONENT: THE REAL WORLD

It's Not Who You Think

In 2009, I walked out of the branch ceremony for our class of army officer candidates, elated and so proud of myself. I had accomplished what I had set out to do when I first enlisted in the army. I had made enough points and was high enough in my class ranking to become an engineer officer. There were only five engineer slots out of 120 candidates, and I got one of them!

When I enlisted in the army, it was a strategic move. I had two soft degrees, both in the realm of political science and leadership. I knew I needed something technical in my education to make me competitive to corporations for when the economy turned around. The Army's Engineer Corps could provide me with the technical side I needed, but it was a risky move. Coming in as an officer candidate, there is a high chance that you don't get your first career choice when you sign the dotted line. But there I was. I picked up my little castle pin off of the table and squirmed in excitement for the remainder of the ceremony.

Following the ceremony, our class gathered outside where congratulations were heard in every direction. In officer candidate school you have two types of candidates, prior service members who were previously enlisted and applied to be officers, and civilians who entered the army as a candidate. I was the latter. During all of our celebrations, one of the prior enlisted candidates approached me with a huge smile and a handshake.

"Callie! I can't believe you're going to be an engineer officer. *That's awesome!* I didn't know you were that hoo-ahh!"

Giggling with excitement, "Thanks! I was so worried I wouldn't get it."

And in a split second I thought "hoo-ahh," what does he mean?

I continued, "What do you mean by hoo-ahh?"

With even more excitement he said, "You're gonna go out there in front of the infantry, in front of everyone and clear roadside bombs! That's some crazy stuff there! I didn't realize you were that crazy!"

The complete excitement turned to complete confusion. I joined the Engineer Corps to build stuff, what did roadside bombs have to do with engineering?

Confused, I asked. "What do you mean? Engineers build things."

He replied, "In these wars, in Iraq and Afghanistan, engineers are mostly combat engineers. They conduct route clearance, going out in front of everyone else to find roadside bombs."

"Wait *what*?!"

"You didn't know that?"

With a look of complete and utter shock, I answered, "*No*... I thought I'd be building stuff."

With a chuckle he replied, "Not likely for these wars. Combat engineers blow sh** up."

He gave me a pat on the back and another handshake before walking away to give more congratulations as I stood there with what was likely a blank stare and panic in my eyes. Did I just make the biggest mistake of my life? This was not how I planned this to go at all!

In every sports game there is an opponent. As this is a playbook, you too have an opponent as you play the Bold Maneuver. You may subconsciously think that the opponent you're going up against is men; that men are the reason you're having to adjust and strategize the way we work. The real opponent, however, is the real world. The real world is hard, it's messy, it's complex. There isn't an easy way to move through a path without struggle or failure. Throughout the book I have mentioned the three rules. The reason these rules are so prevalent is because they are the opponent. When the real world strikes at work and stuff happens, life's not fair, and no one is there to help, it is up to you to move ahead, placing one foot in front of the other, in a positive direction.

I never expected to be in the situation I was when I grabbed that engineer pin at that ceremony. I thought I was going to build things, not blow them up. I had no intention of being a combat arms, no less a combat arms female. My entire life changed after that moment, my path is much different than what it would have been due to the real world turning me on my head.

Guy Troubles

While in a lot of ways we still live and work in a male-dominant society or industry, men are not the enemy. The Bold Maneuver is not to pick apart masculine traits and characteristics, to say that those characteristics are wrong, or say that all of your work problems are because of men. This idea of gender gap, or gender equality is just a part of the larger whole. In so many ways your opponent, the real world, encompasses personalities, not genders. The opponent that stands in the way of your success is other people, just as much as it is you. Everyone carries personality traits that have a positive and negative impact on other people. We have personality traits that have positive and negative impacts on ourselves, creating self-sabotage. Adjusting your perspective from a gender problem set to a personality one will help you be more open and receptive. A lot of my clients have an unconscious bias and perception of men that creates a wall, because they stereotype the average male to be one thing. This behavior is self-sabotaging because it prevents you from seeing the full situation. This is why the One-on-One is so important.

Failures and Mistakes

Are you someone who holds grudges or lets it go? For the longest time I thought I was the latter. I thought I did a pretty good job at forgiving, until I got married. I realized pretty quickly into our marriage that I was the reason behind my own unhappiness. My husband would do something unintentionally that would hurt my feelings or irritate me, we would talk about it, he would genuinely apologize, then in the next tiff, I would bring up his past mistake. Man! How unfair is that?! How would I feel if he used my mistakes or misunderstandings against me?

Just like in our lives outside of work, at work we all make mistakes. Our mistakes may be unintentional or intentional, but either way they have repercussions. We all fail at work, maybe on a small task we forgot, or a large project that was unsuccessful. When it comes to mistakes and failures, letting go is simply the best solution to your success. When you fail or make a mistake, how do you prefer people to react? Do you want them to quickly forget? Maybe quickly forgive, if it had a negative impact directly on them? We all want that, we don't want our failures and mistakes to be the only thing people think of. Reflect, learn, and move on. Become agile in your ability to move forward quickly.

False Reality

The biggest hindrance to western cultures is the belief that bad things shouldn't happen to good people. This is a killer to our society. It kills motivation, action, and ambition. It goes back to that early childhood lesson that if you do the right thing and work hard, you'll be successful. It then hits us like a ton of bricks when we enter our twenties, and we struggle for years with it being a false reality. This is why the gratitude skill becomes imperative to your success. When you are conditioned to see the opportunities within struggles or problems, you are able to overcome the emotion around the issue much more quickly and devise a strategy to maneuver through the situation. This is where the functional fitness conditioning comes in. If you are conditioned to accept unfavorable conditions, know that you are capable of thriving in unfavorable conditions, and have the skills necessary to outmaneuver the opponent, you'll be more successful than you ever imagined.

Real World Rules

The real world is hard! And sometimes it can be downright scary. The unpredictability and uncertainty can be a huge weight. I am with you! Sometimes I struggle with worry, or what-ifs, and my thought spiderwebs can get out of control in a matter of minutes, and that is okay. None of us will ever be perfect in an imperfect world. It is 100 percent okay to have self-doubt, confusion and fear in what you're doing. Your career may feel like it's going off the hinges and spinning out of control without you, maybe it's simply unsatisfying, but those feelings are valid. The goal is not to not feel, or ignore our feelings, but to react in a way that helps us grow and succeed. As much as the real world can provide wonderful surprises, it can be just as discomforting. Becoming strategic in how you react to situations good and bad, is how you achieve the Bold Maneuver.

GAME DAY: DECIDE TO DO IT

At the end of this book, it is game day, and it is up to you to decide if you're going to execute the Bold Maneuver as the strategy to move you toward your dreams. Being **bold** is not a laissez-faire activity, being **bold** means taking action, and not just any action, unconventional action.

You most likely picked up this book because what you have been doing and are doing to get ahead and achieve greater success in your career has not been working. The best way to move past stagnation is divergence; to move and branch out from your current state. Are you ready to be *bold* in your career? You have the ability to take ownership of your path, and you have all of the plays to do so.

You've now learned how to set the foundation for your career with functional fitness. You've discovered that there is a game being played, and the only way to win is to love the game. You have six dynamic plays to move you past conventional action. Are you ready to execute the Bold Maneuver as your career strategy, to achieve all of your aspirations?

In the stories of the sales director who wanted to negotiate a higher salary and the bank manager who wanted to be more engaged in her community, they were both high-achievers unsure of how to move forward. Most of my clients are high-achievers that have had career success, but feel stuck or feel they've got nowhere to go in their career. The truth is there is always a way to move up, it just takes a new perspective and a new approach. With both of these clients, they took action executing the plays and achieved their objectives.

One of the biggest challenges to implementing the Bold Maneuver is throwing the plays aside when you don't see immediate success. These two clients both began to regress to their habitual behavior when they felt uncomfortable with the circumstances around their action. Being bold means you will feel discomfort. Being unconventional is uncomfortable, which is why few people are intentionally unconventional. But... if you continue to play the game and play the plays, you will find the discomfort subsides and an internal power you never knew existed will start to emerge. Not only are you able to hit your near goals, but you will find your career aspirations within reach again and know how to go all the way.

The skills you build from this book and the application of the plays will not only help you in your current efforts, but in your future ones. The goal is to find success, but enjoy the journey; the Bold Maneuver may seem like work now, but when it becomes second nature, you will find joy in the little insights it brings you. These insights are what will make you relevant and unmatched.

I told you in the beginning that strategy can be learned; it isn't as overwhelming now is it? All it means is you are intentional and calculated in your choices, in your actions. So many women let their companies, their bosses, their co-workers determine their success. They unintentionally go with the flow thinking that if they work hard, they will be rewarded and when they aren't they become frustrated with the system. Being strategic is taking ownership of your future, your career, your dreams. What is more powerful than that?

The game is waiting on you, it isn't going anywhere. Are you ready? Now is the time. Are you going to be the next success story, the next woman executive, the next woman CEO? Time to be bold, and play bold with the Bold Maneuver.

ACKNOWLEDGMENTS

Going off on your own to start a business is terrifying.

Chris, you were the first person nudging me to make my own path. Your encouragement, confidence, friendship, partnership, and love make me stronger every day and they are just a few of the things I am most thankful for when it comes to you. Thank you for being my teammate in everything!

To my mother and sister. You two have been my number one fans in all of my adventures. I could not have been gifted more amazing women than the two of you.

To my friend Lauren Enderlein. Thank you or all of those hours spent being my first reader on my first draft, and listening to all of my crazy ideas. You have been such an amazing friend and confidant on this new journey and I truly appreciate all of your encouragement and feedback.

To my family and friends, you know who you are. You are so much of what makes up my foundation. You have been there through it all, and have supported me every step of the way. Thank you for being my tribe, my village.

To Angela, The Author Incubator, for your amazing mentorship on my entrepreneurial journey. I still have no idea how I found you, but I am so thankful you believed in my story and my movement. I could have not done any of this without you!

To the Morgan James Publishing team: Special thanks to David Hancock, CEO & Founder for believing in me and my message. To my Author Relations Manager, Margo Toulouse, thanks for making the process seamless and easy. Many more thanks to everyone else, but especially Jim Howard, Bethany Marshall, and Nickcole Watkins.

Special Thanks to the Book Launch Team

Cassandra Lentz

Marrianne Ryno

Sara Smith

Vera Riley

Sara Cummings

Jennifer Johnson

April Ash

Ashley Nieves-Martinez

Kendall Mealy

Rebecca Loboschefsky

Diane Worrell Clayton

James Long

Jennifer Long

Starre Quinones Hayes

Laci Jo Rains

Cedrick Tardy

Sarah Billings

Emily Eunhye Kim

Brandon Kirch

Marc Cordon

Vanessa Chandler

Angel Rodriguez

Dominique Seldon

Casey Bright

Amber Stevens

Missy Blades Lander

Sam Lubin

Cait Whitmire

Mandy Orr Essex

Chasity Dozier

Anthony Weiss

Chasity Youngblood Reed

Suzie Woodburn

Laci Jo Raines

Shonda Jean Waxman

Nate Dumas

Kendall Stratman Williams

Jenny Henderson

Christina Gabriel

ABOUT THE AUTHOR

 Callie Cummings is dedicated to helping women become sought after leaders in their organizations and fields. She founded The Bold Maneuver, a coaching and consulting business, after a second tour in Afghanistan. Having spent over two years in a country where failing human rights against women is ever present, she resolved to help women become power players so they can make the changes they see are needed in their lives and work.

The majority of her professional career occurred within male dominant workforces where she became accustomed to being the only woman on the team. With a M.A. in Global Leadership and Sustainable Development and leadership experience spanning international development and government intelligence, her journey to becoming a best selling author and success coach is one that involves surfboards and bombs, and a little of everything in-between.

Callie is a master systems thinker who has built her repertoire in the financial, tech, and defense industries. She went from working on Wall Street, to becoming an Army Engineer Officer responsible for clearing roadside bombs in Afghanistan, to redesigning a global brand portfolio for a Fortune 100.

At a time when women in combat zones is still being debated, She is am among a small group of women to have lead ground combat troops during an overseas combat tour and proven the abilities and positive outcomes of women on the front lines for future generations.

Working with clients, locally, nationally, and abroad, she helps women become strategists and influencers in their industries, paving the way for future generations of girls.

www.TheBoldManeuver.com

callie@TheBoldManeuver.com

@TheBoldManeuver

THANK YOU

Look at you! Getting to this point in the book means that you are ready to make amazing, career defining, Bold Maneuvers.

As with most new concepts we encounter, we come to the point where we are ready to put the skills we learned into play; only to find out it's very different to put those skills into action in our everyday lives than it is to read about it.

To support your Bold Maneuver journey, I have developed two quizzes to get you started.

The first quiz, What Bold Maneuver Play Do You Need To Be Playing, determines which of the six Bold Maneuver plays you should start with based on your present situation and needs. You can take this quiz by going to The Bold Maneuver website, www.theboldmaneuver.com/quiz.

The second quiz, What Is Your Strongest Bold Maneuver Play, identifies which of the plays in the playbook is your strongest. You may prefer one play over another, but this quiz is a fun way to identify which one you're best at playing. You can take this quiz by going to The Bold Maneuver website, www.theboldmaneuver.com/strengths.

To achieve greatness in work and life, we must make Bold Maneuvers! As you start your Bold Maneuver journey, keep in mind that all of the fun and the love of the game comes with you being bolder than you think you are, and more importantly, bolder than everyone else thinks you are!

Connect with Callie at www.TheBoldManeuver.com or info@TheBoldManeuver.com

Morgan James
Speakers Group

www.TheMorganJamesSpeakersGroup.com

We connect Morgan James published authors with live and online events and audiences who will benefit from their expertise.